ALSO BY WILLIAM MARES

The Marine Machine

Passing Brave
(with William Polk)

Working Together
(with John Simmons)

Real Vermonters Don't Milk Goats
(with Frank Bryan)

MAKING BEER

MAKING BEER

By William Mares

ILLUSTRATED BY JEFF DANZIGER

Alfred A. Knopf   NEW YORK   1992

ACKNOWLEDGMENTS

Many persons helped and encouraged me in writing this book. In particular I want to thank Pat Baker, Tom Burns, Fred Eckhardt, Ken Grossman, Stuart Harris, Michael Jackson, Prof. Michael Lewis, Fritz Maytag,
Steve Morris, Bill Owens, Charlie Papazian, George Peppard, Ed Quillen,
and Jim Schleuter.

Library of Congress Cataloging in Publication Data

Mares, William.   Making beer.

Bibliography: p.
1. Beer. 2. Brewing. I. Title.
TP577.M337 1984   641.8′73   83-48868
ISBN 0-394-72328-7 (pbk.)

Manufactured in the United States of America

Published April 26, 1984
Reprinted Five Times
Seventh Printing, March 1992

For my father,
who first told me about home brew,
and my wife, Chris,
who helped improve both my beer
and my prose

Contents

Preface

This book traces the evolution of a hobby, that of brewing my own beer. Over a ten-year period, this hobby first tempted, then seduced, and finally abducted me. I now make about 120 gallons of lagers, ales, and stouts each year. I am the president of the Vermont Home Brewers Association and the state dark-ale champion. I love the challenge and variety of brewing. At any one time I have ten to twenty cases of different beers aging in the basement. Shamelessly, I foist my brews on guests or bring them to dinner parties as gifts. I will turn the talk to beer at the first opportunity. Thus, some would say the following definition deftly describes my home brewing: "Hobby—an individual pursuit to which a person is devoted (in the speaker's opinion) out of proportion to its real importance" (*Oxford Universal Dictionary*).

I don't use lightly such words as *tempt* and *seduce*. They are appropriate for one raised under the brooding tutelage of John Calvin to believe that work is sacred, that the idle mind is the devil's playground, and, if I may use a twentieth-century metaphor, that vacations are merely pit stops in the race of life.

H. L. Mencken, himself an avid home brewer during Prohibition, once described a Calvinist as a person in whose heart lurks the haunting fear that someone somewhere just might be having a good time. And drinking beer certainly means having a good time.

Learning to brew enabled me to have my moral hardtack and eat it too: it exacted enough mortification through failure to satisfy my Calvinism, while eventually rewarding me with success and the pleasure of drinking and sharing my own creations with friends. It is better to give than to receive, I know, but there is also nothing wrong with receiving praise in return for a labor of love.

WILLIAM MARES
Burlington, Vermont

MAKING BEER

A Fateful Glass
of Home Brew

My home brewing really began with a bagpipe lesson.

Knowing of my delight in pipe music, my father bought a used set of pipes in England for my college graduation present. For the next few weeks, I made desultory attempts to learn the fingering and play simple tunes on the chanter. I couldn't get a squeak out of the pipes themselves, though, and I soon gave up.

Not until ten years later, when Chris and I moved to Vermont and hired a piper to play at our wedding, did I feel the urge to try the pipes again. Our house was far enough out in the country so that the pagan wailings were but antiphonal to the dogs' and coyotes' howling, but it was obvious that I needed help. After a few inquiries, I learned of a Scott Hastings (surely a promising name), a museum curator and piper who performed around the state.

At his home in Taftsville, Hastings looked over my pipes, took them under his arm, and tuned them for five minutes. Then he made the room reverberate with primitive, spine-tingling melodies. "These pipes are okay," he said, "but they won't play themselves. Playing the pipes is not like raising corn or bees, you know. You have to work at it every day."

As we prepared to leave, he asked almost in passing, "Would you like to try a home-brewed beer?"

At that, his wife, Elsie, suddenly came into focus. While we had been intent on the music, she had been working at the sink, washing out several dozen brown beer bottles. On a chair nearby sat a green garbage can covered with a piece of cheesecloth. Elsie made four or five five-gallon (two-case) batches of home brew each year, and this was bottling day for the latest batch.

Scott disappeared into the basement and returned with a label-less quart bottle. When he pried off the plain cap, the gentle hiss was barely audible. He poured the contents into three glasses until the last portion turned cloudy. It looked like regular beer with its clear, golden color and white, foamy head. It smelled something like beer, mixed with a tinge of cider. I took a sip. It didn't taste exactly like beer. It was both fuller and sharper than the brands I was used to drinking. It had a strong but pleasant aftertaste, sharp but not bitter, quite pleasant.

My only prior exposure to home brew had been secondhand. Like millions of Americans, my father had made home brew during Prohibition. He told me of an experience which was probably repeated thousands of times during those thirteen years of national hypocrisy. He was living in Akron, Ohio, where he worked as a chemist for Goodyear Tire and Rubber Co. He did his brewing in the bathroom and then stored the beer in a closet of his second-floor apartment.

One hot summer's afternoon, the landlady called him at work to say that his beer was exploding and some of it had already leaked through the floor of his apartment. By the time he got home, most of the bottles had burst, the landlady's couch was soaked, and her mood was dark indeed. If he paid for the repairs and cleaning, and promised not to brew again, he could stay. He complied.

It is hard to grow up in Texas without drinking a lot of beer. On the Gulf Coast where I lived, humid 90° F. weather was possible nine to ten months of the year. In contrast to Vermont, which has "eleven months of winter and one month of damned poor sledding," Texas has ten months of summer and two months of spent "northers" which bring ducks and a touch of frost. In consequence, I always seemed to be thirsty. For Texans, beer is the liquid complement to seafood, barbecue, fried chicken, and, most of all, Mexican food. Like all my friends, I was no beer connoisseur. My favorites were Bud, Miller, and Busch. I scorned regional beers like Lone Star, Pearl, Jax, and Shiner.

I applied to Harvard in part because of Guinness Stout. When I went east to visit colleges in my senior year, my brother, then at Harvard, took me to Cronin's, a popular saloon off Harvard Square. Amid the smoke, vivacious conversation, tweed jackets, and crossed rowing oars, he treated me to my first creamy, black, bittersweet Guinness. Now this was the college life for me: study all day and drink Guinness into the night.

In Texas I learned to drink beer; at Harvard I learned to hold and appreciate it. On four of the first six Saturdays of my freshman year, I got drunk. I was not lonely, I was not depressed, but no one in the dorm seemed to know any girls, and our way of having fun was to drink Budweiser quarts from the corner liquor store. We varied the routine once or twice by holding contests to see who could down a twelve-ounce can the fastest. The time I won, I did it in 2.3 seconds by cutting two holes in one side of the can and one hole in the other.

But the prizes and wages of our beer blasts were so much retching and wretchedness that I came to hate Sundays and thus moderated my drinking. In those days, American beer was beer was beer. There might have been some differences between Budweiser, Miller, and Schlitz, but they were lost on me.

As it turned out, I didn't drink as much Guinness as I had expected. For special occasions, perhaps twice a semester, we went to the Wursthaus, another Harvard Square watering hole that specialized in foreign beers. But they were too expensive to be dangerously habit forming for me.

After college, when I worked in Chicago, Jimmy's Woodlawn Tap became my "local," as the English say. Jimmy's, at the corner of Fifty-fifth Street and Woodlawn Avenue, was the only building to survive a wave of urban renewal that swept through Hyde Park in the 1950s. The dirty, one-story building had no sign of distinction except for the name embossed on the window. It had none of the polished oak, etched glass, or Victorian decoration that seems to grace most bars near universities.

In 1965, steins of Schlitz and hamburgers were 35 cents each. Bottled beer was 50 or 60 cents. Jimmy had Guinness, Bass, Tuborg, and Heineken. My favorite was Special Export from G. Heileman in Wisconsin. It had a hoppy yet sweetish quality that set it off from the bland monotony of the national brands, and it offered the taste of imported beer at a domestic price.

Jimmy's provided the solid connection between good company and good beer. Beer was the drink of moderation and stimulating conversation. My friends did not drink beer to get drunk. If they wanted to get smashed, they went for the hard stuff.

My other favorite watering hole in Chicago (until it closed in 1967) was the Sieben Brewery just off Armitage Avenue. Built in 1865, it was both a *Bierstube* and a beer garden. I spent many summer nights sitting in the garden downing steins of Sieben's lager. Sieben did his best to keep the brewery going, but he suffered from declining sales, the competition from the majors, and the dissolution of the solid German neighborhood that had supported the brewery for so long. In the 1960s that was enough to kill off dozens of breweries like Sieben's. There were just too few beer aficionados who understood that the major brands offered nothing better than Sieben's except flashier advertising.

I discovered the enormous variety and complexity of beer on travels abroad. As a member of the Harvard Glee Club, I toured the Far East, and after concerts I savored such marvels as Kirin, Asahi, Sapporo, San Miguel, Singha, and Golden Eagle. During a half year I spent studying in Germany, I drank my fill of Spaten Bräu, genuine Löwenbrau, Hacker Bräu, and seemingly dozens of local beers across Bavaria, Swabia, and the Palatinate.

Later, my work as a journalist took me to Europe and Africa. Our visit to Scott Hastings came a few months after a six-week trip to Ghana, where Chris and I consumed gallons of Club, Star, and locally made Guinness, all full bodied and refreshing. Each time I returned to the United States, I was more disappointed with the beers offered by our big brewers. I was struck by the blandness, the icy temperature, and the hard-edged fizziness of them all.

I saw that emulating Elsie Hastings would give me a chance to avoid the big brewers. I would create my own beer at a reasonable cost and brew whatever variety I could imagine. Home brewing fit in well with the other strains of self-sufficiency our friends were then practicing in Vermont: sheep raising, beekeeping, vegetable gardening, and the like. That brewing was technically illegal only added to its appeal.

It was several months before I could assemble the necessary equipment from local hardware stores. I bought a 10-gallon green plastic garbage can, a capper, and a gross of caps. At a grocery store, I picked up a can of Blue Ribbon Hopped Malt Extract, five pounds of sugar, several packets of Fleischmann's baker's yeast, and some cheesecloth.

My father gave me a recipe which said to boil a gallon of water, pour in the malt syrup and sugar, boil ten to fifteen minutes, and then add four gallons of tap water to cool the brew to 80° F. Then I was to sprinkle in the yeast. I used a cross-country ski thermometer to measure that final temperature. To keep the flies out of the garbage can as the brew fermented, I draped two thicknesses of cheesecloth over the top and tied it securely. This still permitted me to watch the fermentation's progress. My father had said nothing about cleaning the bottles, so I just washed them out with soapy water, rinsed them, and let them stand.

Faithfully I followed his instructions. However, he didn't tell me that malt syrup had the consistency of 90-weight engine oil. Which meant that as I brought the liquid back to a boil, some of the undissolved syrup stuck to the bottom of the pot and burned. Undeterred, I pressed on. I assumed that since the yeast was to be added at 80° F., the ambient temperature should remain close to that, so I kept the can in front of a window where it was 75° F. during the day.

After about eight hours, a thin film had formed on the surface. The next day the froth was about an inch deep and looked like dirty shaving cream. It did smell something like beer, though heavy on the carbon dioxide. My father said to let it perk until the head dropped and most of the bubbles disappeared, which should take four or five days.

The head eventually rose to a height of two inches, and then, as he predicted, it subsided. Or rather, collapsed. In one day it fell and disappeared. Since I could still see tiny bubbles rising to the surface, I decided to let the mixture ferment for two more days. After that, no further bubbles were evident. In their place, there appeared miniature lily pads of white moldy material about half an inch across. These were completely unexpected and didn't appear to belong in the beer, so I took a kitchen sieve and skimmed off as many as I could.

After a week I decided it was bottling time. I carefully spooned a teaspoon of sugar into each bottle to give the beer the necessary carbonation. Then I took a length of plastic hose, held one end in the brew

and put my finger over the other end. I sucked out some of the beer to create a gravity feed. It tasted a bit sharp, but not rancid. I assumed that the sugar in the bottles would even out the taste.

I managed to fill fifty bottles and only spilled a quart or so on the floor. I capped the bottles, put them in two cases, and grandly marked the boxes HOME BREW. I carried the cases to the basement and stored them in the coolest corner.

That seemed simple enough.

About a week later we were having breakfast when Chris asked me if I had heard a jet break the sound barrier during the night. I hadn't.

I didn't miss the second salvo.

As I was washing the dishes, there came a loud *crumpp!* from the basement, followed by the soft tinkling of glass. We didn't need some fancy problem-analysis to understand what was happening: the beer was exploding. The problem now was damage control. Should we leave the bottles there to commit suicide in peace if not quiet? They were next to the washing machine and we'd have to do a laundry sometime during the next week. Should I go down there now and cover the cases with planks of wood? That would mean that eventually all five gallons of beer would end up on the floor and shards of glass would be everywhere.

I decided I had to get the beer outside. So I bundled up in a heavy winter parka and put on Chris's ski goggles and a plastic helmet. Thick mittens and hiking boots completed my armor. While I was dressing, another bottle blew. I found a piece of half-inch plywood about the dimensions of a beer case. With this shield, I sallied down into the basement. The air was thick with the sweetish smell of spilt beer. I sneaked around an oil tank and quickly placed my shield on top of the first case. Gently, I wiggled my fingers under it and made my way upstairs. Only then did I realize I had no protection under my chin. Another explosion might send a cap flying up through the wood to penetrate my lower jaw. Too late for such worries now.

I carried the case out to the barn and put it down in a stall. Mission half accomplished. I was sweating like a pig as I went back for the second case.

Once both cases were safely transported, I felt I just had to try one of those beers. I took an opener back to the barn. Squatting to one side, I raised the lid on a case and extracted a bottle. With its top pointed away from me, I slowly pulled off the cap. With a great hiss, white foam spewed out of the bottle. As this pocket volcano gushed forth, I took the first and last sip of my maiden batch of home brew. It tasted like liquid, carbonated, sweetish, over-yeasty bread dough.

Back in the house, I stripped off my soaking armor. Whoever said you can't build up a thirst by 9:00 a.m. was wrong. I pulled out a Piels, popped the top with sudden respect for professional brewers, and sat down to watch the sun burn off the early morning fog. Even as I drew my first deep swallow, another bottle exploded down in the barn.

For the next two weeks the beer continued to lay down harassing fire, lobbing scornful shells into my enthusiasm. Perhaps I should stick to bagpipes and bees. The former required only practice, and the stings of the latter seemed an acceptable price to pay for the sweetness of the honey.

It was not an auspicious beginning for a successful home brewer.

A Quick History
of Home Brewing

In the beginning, all brew was home brew. The exact origins of beer are unclear, but the earliest records we have of fermented beverages come from the Tigris-Euphrates valley eight thousand years before Christ was born.

No one knows when the first Sumerian peasant happened upon the idea of soaking hard barley kernels in water to soften them for eating. Similarly, no one can tell when the next peasant in that apostolic succession of home brewers deliberately or inadvertently left some of those soaked grains to dry, chewed on them, and discovered a delightful nutty and slightly sweet flavor. And finally, it is not clear when the next peasant ground those grains for bread and found that when soaked in water for several days the bread magically transformed the water into something not only drinkable but transporting.

Cuneiform records document brewing in Mesopotamia by 6000 B.C. using a variety of barleys and wheats. In time, about 40 percent of the Sumerian barley crop was devoted to beer production, and wages and salaries were often paid partly in beer.

The priesthood soon realized that people were reaching an altered state of consciousness by drinking beer, so they made haste to sanctify the potion and give it its own goddess, Ninkasi, "the lady who fills the mouth." At the same time, commercial breweries sprang up to slake the thirst of those who could not brew their own.

In his book *The Sumerians,* Samuel N. Kramer writes of Ninkasi:

"Although she was a goddess, born in sparkling-fresh water," it was beer that was her first love. She is described in a hymn of glorification addressed to her by one of the devotees of the Inanna cult as the brewer of the gods who "bakes with lofty shovel the sprouted barley; who mixes the happir-malt with sweet aromatics; who bakes the happir-malt in the lofty bin; and who pours the fragrant beer in the lahtan-vessel which is like the Tigris and Euphrates joined."

In the year 2500 B.C., one cuneiform text contained a long list of different words for beer, including dark beer, whitish kuran-beer, reddish beer, excellent beer, beer (mixed) of two parts, beer from the "Nether-World," beer with a head, beer which has been diluted, beer which has been clarified, beer for the sacrifice and beer for the main (divine) repast.

Meanwhile, the art of brewing was also developing in Egypt. There, beer was looked upon as a gift of the god Osiris and was an integral part of festivals and ceremonies. In Egypt, beermaking grew directly out of breadmaking. A dough of sprouted, ground grains was partly baked, then torn apart and soaked in water for a day or two, during which time (we now know) fermentation by wild yeasts occurred. The "liquor" was strained off and the beer was ready to drink. Of course, no one knew what yeast was or how it acted on the grain sugars; but in time, brewers realized that when some of the lees of previous batches were added to a new one, the fermentation went faster.

These ancient brewers were not content with the same brew week in and week out. They experimented constantly with different flavors, spices, such as ginger and juniper, and herbs to vary the taste. With the priesthood involved, these "experiments" had strong religious and magical overtones. Beer became the national drink of Egypt. To give a party was to "arrange a house of beer."

Early brewers doubtless had plenty of failures, given the unscientific nature of the process. The Egyptians passed their brewing knowledge on to the Greeks, who in turn carried the brews to the Romans, although both those northern Mediterranean peoples preferred wine.

Meanwhile, the tribes roaming northern Europe were settling down long enough to learn to make beer using native grains, honey, and, later, barley. As early as 2000 B.C. the "beaker people" were producing and selling beer. Early Danes brewed a cross between wine and beer with barley, cranberries, and bog myrtle. The Roman historian Tacitus wrote of Germans who drank a barley-wheat beer spiced with ginger, anise, or juniper.

In medieval England most large households had their own brewing operations. The brewers (and malters) tended to be women, hence the names *maltster* and *brewster*. The beers varied in strength from the equivalent of near beer to strong barley wines. The northern European peasantry generally drank large quantities of low-alcohol beer in the manner and for the same reason that nineteenth-century New England farmers consumed hard cider—it was safer than the water.

Hops, the viny source of modern beer's pleasant bitterness, was only one of many flavors added to beer until the eighth or ninth century A.D. After that, there are records of the continuous use of hops in Bavarian beer. By the end of the fifteenth century, hops had become barley's inseparable partner in most Continental beers.

The introduction of hops into England, however, caused a furor. Lovers of unhopped ale fought a rearguard action against the Dutch hops that had gained a foothold of cultivation in Kent. In fact, Henry VIII banned their importation, but by the end of the sixteenth century the English marriage of hops and barley malt was generally accepted.

Thus the term *ale*, which originally distinguished English beer from hopped Continental beer, came to mean top-fermented (and hopped) English-style brew in contrast to the bottom-fermented (lager) variety. Hopped beer seems to have won the day because of its excellent preservative and sterilizing qualities in addition to its ability to balance the malt. (In the rest of this book, I have adopted the English custom of referring to both beer and ale as "beer." When Shakespeare wrote, "I will make it felony to drink small beer," he meant ale. When I say "ale," I will mean the top-fermented beer.)

The first white settlers in North America brought with them both commercial and home brewing. The Jamestown colony made a poor beer out of Indian corn. The Pilgrims at Plymouth, according to the diary of one of their members, were in distress because they "could not now take time for further search or consideration, our victuals being much spent, especially Beere."

John Alden, a cooper by trade and caretaker of the *Mayflower's* beer barrels, decided to settle in the new land with the immigrants when he saw their need for beer.

Beer was a staple in the Puritans' diet, as testified by this passage from the diary of minister Richard Mather in 1635: "And a speciall means of ye healthfulnesse of ye passengers by ye blessing of God wee all conceyved to bee much walking in ye open ayre, and ye comfortable variety of our food; . . . we had no want of good and wholesome beere and bread."

In 1630, the year my mother's ancestors came to America from England, one ship, the *Arabella*, left port carrying three times as much beer as water.

Pastors and public officials praised the benefits of beer because it provided a stout defense against the ravages of "strong waters," a euphemism for Demon Rum.

In 1635, within six years of the establishment of the West India Company colony on Manhattan, its Dutch inhabitants had built their first brewery. English and Dutch brewers and home brewers had to weigh the expense and time of securing ingredients from Europe against the search for local sources of supply. The wealthy continued to import beer from Europe, but anyone living even a few miles from the port cities soon turned to his own devices. Home brewing was not a hobby but a necessity.

The colonists used wild hops when they could find them, or substituted ground ivy and juniper berries. One of the most popular alternatives was essence of red or black spruce, which also worked well as a preventative against scurvy.

> *If barley be wanting to make into malt*
> *We must be content and think it no fault*
> *For we can make liquor to sweeten our lips*
> *Of pumpkins, and parsnips, and walnut-tree chips.*

As Mark E. Lender, a modern writer on American drinking habits, put it: "One suspects that the beers produced from such recipes were little better than the poetry."

Like their English forebears, early American settlers brewed roughly three classes of beer according to strength. The weakest and most commonly drunk was called small beer. At the other end of the spectrum was strong beer, so defined by the length of time the malt was soaked in water to convert starches into fermentable sugars. Strong beer, which might have 6 to 7 percent alcohol, was a favorite of the wealthier classes who could usually afford to have an in-house brewer. In between was middle beer, or table beer.

All these beers were cloudy, an aesthetic fact traceable to the top-fermenting yeast which had evolved in England. One reason for the popularity of hard cider among the colonial elite was that in contrast to beers of all strengths, the cider was clear. As beer historian Stanley Baron wrote in *Brewed in America*: "The most characteristic aspect of brewing in the seventeenth century, however, was its chanciness. Brewers understood very little about the technology of their trade, and the chemistry involved was beyond them. Measuring devices, such as the thermometer and hydrometer, did not come into practical use until the second half of the eighteenth century. Everything about their brewing was inaccurate and capricious; they could not explain why one brew came out well and the next poorly. The properties and control of yeast remained unexplored until the researches of Pasteur and Hansen in the 1870's. No wonder we find frequent references to 'the art and mystery of brewing.' "

Harvard owned three breweries in succession in the seventeenth and early eighteenth centuries, and beer, or its lack, figured in the dismissal of the college's first president. Under the terms of matriculation, President Nathaniel Eaton and his wife were to provide the students with a weekly ration of bread and beer. According to S. E. Morison, in the bill of particulars brought against Eaton, college authorities alleged, and Eaton's wife admitted, that the promised beer was sometimes "wanting . . . a week or half a week together."

Baron suggests that one of the first recorded recipes for home brewing in North America was written by George Washington:

To Make Small Beer

Take a large Siffer [Sifter] full of Bran Hops to your Taste. Boil these 3 hours then strain out 30 Gallons into a Cooler put in 3 Gallons Molasses while the Beer is Scalding hot or rather draw the Melasses into the Cooler & St[r]ain the Beer on it while boiling Hot. Let this stand till it is little more than Blood warm then put in a quart of Yea[s]t if the Weather is very Cold cover it over with a Blank[et] & let it Work in the Cooler 24 hours then put it into the Cask—leave the Bung [Stopper] open till it is almost don[e] Working—Bottle it that day Week it was Brewed."

In his retirement, the polymath Thomas Jefferson turned to brewing with characteristic thoroughness. Baron quotes his answer to an inquiry about private brewing from James Madison:

Our brewing for the use of the present year has been some time over. About the last of Oct. or beginning of Nov. we begin for the ensuing year, and malt and brew three sixty gallon casks . . . in as much as you will want a house of Malting, which is quickest made by digging into the steep side of a hill, so as to need a roof only, and you will want a hair cloth also of the size of your loft to lay the grain in. This can only be had from Philadelphia or New York. . . . I will give you notice in the fall when we are to commence malting and our malter and brewer is uncommonly intelligent and capable of giving instruction if your pupil is as ready at comprehending it.

The differences in technique between home brewing and commercial brewing were not great, even into the nineteenth century. Until Pasteur's isolation of yeast culture, both had to rely upon the careful extraction and retention of the lees in which rested the yeast from the previous batch.

By the beginning of the nineteenth century, there were some 132 breweries in the United States, producing 285,000 barrels annually. (In the same year, a single London brewery, The Anchor, made 205,000 barrels.)

In 1840, a Philadelphia brewer named John Wagner brought some bottom-fermenting yeast from Germany to his small establishment on St. John Street. There, in a kettle hung over an open hearth, he brewed eight barrels of beer, which were subsequently stored (lagered) in the cellar. (*Lagern* in German means "to store.") From these humble beginnings arose the wave of lager beer, which by 1880 had engulfed the country.

Before 1840, all beers drunk in the United States were top-fermented ales, porters, and stouts. After 1880 over 90 percent of the beer was bottom-fermented lager. There were several reasons for the switch. First, the highly carbonated lager was more thirst quenching in the hotter climate of the United States. Second, it was clearer and its introduction coincided with the invention of cheap, transparent glass in which to serve the beer. Third, the failed German revolution of 1848 sent thousands of discontented emigrants to the New World. Some of them were brewers, and almost all were lager drinkers. Germans set up hundreds of local and regional breweries in the following years. So ubiquitous were these breweries and so good were their products, that fewer and fewer people bothered to brew their own. One authority on the history of American food, Richard J. Hooker, also suggests that lighter-bodied lagers were more compatible with Americans' relatively high meat diet.

The need for refrigeration both in the manufacture and storage of lager made it next to impossible for home brewers to match the store-bought or saloon beer. Home brewing became the province of a few cranks and those isolated on the frontier. People who lived scores of miles from the nearest brewery used recipes not unlike this one from the Australian outback, courtesy of Ian McDonald:

4 lbs. white sugar	3 oz. hops
1 tsp. dry baker's yeast	2 gals. water
1 lb. brown sugar	1 tsp. salt
2 lbs. Saunders Malt extract	

Boil 1 gal. of water in enamel bucket, add hops tied in bag and make it sit down and soak. Boil 20 minutes, take bag out. Squeeze out as soon as cool and put back into brew. While bag is cooling, add all other ingredients except yeast. When everything has dissolved, add the other gallon of water. Stick finger in at blood heat, add yeast at this temperature.

Put bucket in warmest place, possibly a cupboard, and cover with a towel to let air in. Don't move around.

Skim off froth and flies. Leave approximately 7 days in warm place, until top clears and sediment drops. Siphon into another container, anything, wash out sediment, and pour back into bucket. Leave another 24 hours to settle again. Siphon again and then bottle one-third full. Top up with clean water.

Soak bottle tops in water beforehand to wet cork for one half hour. Cap the bottles. Store bottles standing up in a cool place. Start drinking after a fortnight—preferably a month. Must be cold.

Home brewing returned to the United States under duress. On January 16, 1920, Prohibition became law and millions of citizens like my father became lawbreakers. Offended equally by the law and the bootleggers' prices, would-be brewers had to start from scratch. There were no recipe books and certainly no home brew supply shops selling ingredients and equipment. Most home brewers had to rely upon the imperfect and often foggy memories of their own fathers.

Their chief inspiration was Lena, the round and warm-faced woman who graced the label of the Blue Ribbon malt can manufactured by Pabst. Fortunately, malt could still be sold because of its use in baking.

When home brewers couldn't find Lena, they resorted to all kinds of alternatives, such as corn, rice, and wheat. By and large, the result was powerful, cidery, cloudy, and tolerable only because of the alcohol it contained.

Ed deBenedetti, part owner of a home brew supply store in Portland, Oregon, described his Prohibition brewing:

"We would take a carton of malt, three pounds of sugar and a package of Fleischmann's cake yeast. We used stone jars—six gallons for a five-gallon batch and twelve gallons for a ten-gallon batch. It usually fermented for one week in the crock. Sometimes you'd put light bulbs around it to force it, but if you had a cool basement and it fermented slowly, it made a better beer.

"We'd use two and a half pounds of malt. Bring your water to a rolling boil, put your hops in, and bring it down to a simmer for about twenty minutes. That would be the best brew. When it cooled down a little bit, you added your yeast and it would foam up in the first day or two. You could skim that off, but it wasn't necessary. You boiled the whole batch at once. Lots of people couldn't be bothered to boil: they'd just mix it up. Then, depending on your patience, it would be about two weeks before you drank it. Sometimes it was good, most of the time, it was terrible. I always had pretty good luck.

"Everybody claimed they made the best beer in town. They would make it so darn strong—they would double up on the malt, and the sugar would all ferment out. They would get a high hydrometer reading, but it wouldn't all turn into alcohol because the yeast can only eat so much sugar. You'd have to give it a second shot of yeast. You would have to have the right temperature—sixty to seventy degrees. It was called a warm fermentation."

Beer drinkers came out of Prohibition with both an enormous thirst and a violent distaste for home brew. The commercial breweries were more than happy to welcome them back with a clear, predictable, inoffensive beer that didn't bite. Drinkers were in no mood to talk about the fine points of beer: they wanted to know and see what they were drinking, and they wanted to drink a lot of it.

In 1876, there were over 2,600 brewing companies in the United States. This number fell to 1,100 by 1919. Just over 700 breweries reopened at the end of Prohibition fourteen years later. By 1976, fewer than 40 brewing companies remained. The reduction in numbers was matched by a similar narrowing of beer styles as brewers formulated beers according to the lowest common denominator principle. In a nation bubbling with ethnic diversity, breweries opted for blandness over distinctiveness, inoffensiveness over pleasure, advertising over ingredients, and adjuncts over barley.

In the 1930s a few regional brewers began to explore national distribution. To ship their beers from Milwaukee or St. Louis cost an extra "premium," which was added to the local distributor's price. Through the wonders of modern marketing, the brewers were able to convince the public that the premium was an indication of goodness, not a noun describing an extra cost. Hence the term *premium* beers. In fact, many of the local beers tasted better than the national ones, but they were overshadowed by the so-called premium brands from breweries that were also able to foot the tremendous costs of national advertising.

Another reason for the "lightening" of American beers was the marketing decision during and after World War II to appeal to women, who were thought to prefer a milder taste. The growth of the take-home market, the packaging of beer in cans, and their ready availability in supermarkets also meant that more and more the decision of which beer to buy was being made by women.

In the 1960s the Peter Hand Brewing Company in Chicago introduced Meister Brau Lite and the Gablinger Brewery in New York offered a similar low-calorie beer. They sold modestly well, but were hampered by small advertising budgets. It required the resources of a cigarette maker, Philip Morris, to change the face of American beer. Philip Morris acquired Meister Brau and its Lite label in 1972. Using the weight and sophistication of a massive advertising campaign, Miller moved from seventh to second place among U.S. brewers (behind Anheuser-Busch) and from 5 million barrels to 31 million barrels in sales. Their slogan became "All you ever wanted in a beer. And less." It was a stunning marketing success, one which Budweiser did not take seriously until Miller Lite had already captured over 40 percent of the low-calorie market. By 1980, low-cal beers accounted for 22 percent of total American beer sales.

Not everyone welcomed or accepted the homogenization of beer. Students, servicemen and others who had tasted good beers abroad came home to the sameness of most American brews. The health-consciousness and do-it-yourself movements merged to spawn a breed of people who cared more about what they ate and drank and had the time to prepare that better fare. Some of them were incensed that beer and wine remained the only major food products exempt from federal ingredients—listing requirements. Finally, there were tens of thousands of people who still, quietly, made their own beer in the old-fashioned Prohibition manner, despite home brewing's assumed illegality.

When Prohibition ended, the government specifically legalized the home manufacture and consumption of wine, up to two hundred gallons per two-person household, but it said nothing about beer. For the next forty years, therefore, the public assumed that home brewing was still illegal, although there were no known cases of prosecution for it. Wine supply stores and a number of mail order seed catalogues began to offer some home brew supplies in the late 1960s and early '70s.

Some of the more enterprising and intrepid winemaking supply stores began to import English malt syrups and extracts such as John

Bull, Edme, and Munton & Fison for making beer. The English malting companies, having saturated their domestic markets, looked to the Americans for additional sales. They provided recipes for English ales, stouts, and porters, as well as lagers. Most home brewers were primarily interested in making something that in any case would be clearly different from American beers.

In 1977–1978, an amalgam of California home brewers, led by writer Lee Coe and members of such clubs as the Redwood Lagers, the Maltose Falcons, and the San Andreas Malts, persuaded Senator Alan Cranston to sponsor a bill giving home brewing the same legal status as winemaking. The bill was passed by both houses of Congress and signed by President Carter in 1979.

The key provision of the bill read:

> Beer For Personal or Family Use—Subject to regulation prescribed by the Secretary of the Treasury, any adult may, without payment of tax, produce beer for personal or family use and not for sale. The aggregate amount of beer exempt from tax under this subsection with respect to any household shall not exceed—(1) 200 gallons per calendar year if there are 2 or more adults in such household or (2) 100 gallons per calendar year if there is only 1 adult in such household.

Another ingredient in this beer revolution was the rising demand for imported beers. For years, Heineken led the imports, controlling as much as 40 percent of the market (as it still did in 1981). But millions of Americans were now traveling abroad and bringing home pleasant memories of dozens of other brands, including San Miguel from the Philippines, Dos Equis from Mexico, and Fischer's from France. Imported beer sales rose over 700 percent during the decade of the 1970s. Still, that amounted at most to 2.4 percent of the total U.S. beer consumption. In northern Vermont, Molson and Moosehead became so popular that most people stopped thinking of them as imports.

The American beer industry was in turmoil over style, taste and concentration. It was bisected by seemingly conflicting trends: one group of consumers appeared to want blander, weaker, less distinctive beers— the low-calorie offerings. But another segment demanded heavier, more flavorful, fuller-bodied beers, which were now being marketed as "super-premiums," and the imports. Squeezed in the middle were the regular beers and the smaller regional breweries.

As the major brewers fought each other for a larger market share, they played corporate "Pac Man," devouring one brewery after another until it appeared as if the end of the 1980s would see what Russell Cleary, president of G. Heileman & Co., called a "duopoly" of Anheuser-Busch and Miller.

And where were the home brewers in all this? "Without measurable impact," according to a spokesman for the U.S. Brewers Association.

From Mother Earth
to the Heartland
and Back

I couldn't give up brewing after one try. If my bagpiping could improve, so could my beermaking. What's more, I had grandly told many friends that my beer would be better than anything they had ever tasted before. It was a way to set myself apart from the talents of fly-fishermen, carpenters, poets, and stone masons. To quit after one attempt would be mortifying, although I was beginning to realize that brewing was not as easy as I had anticipated.

My father's advice, when he heard of my explosive failure, was to add less sugar. He pointed out that fermentation has two byproducts—alcohol and carbon dioxide. The bottles probably blew up because I hadn't completed the fermentation and there was no place for the CO_2 to go.

This time I wrote down every step in my procedure, including the fact that I used two-thirds the previous amount of sugar. I also made one small methodological advance: instead of spooning out one teaspoon of sugar into each bottle, I dissolved the whole amount (about a cup) in hot water and then added the solution to the five gallons of brew just before bottling.

When this batch was bottled, I took it directly to the barn and for the next two weeks checked the cases daily. No explosions, so that was progress. I waited another week before trying some. Wearing my goggles,

but not the overcoat, I retrieved one bottle. To reduce the chances of a gusher, I put it in the freezer for a couple of hours. Then I took it outside and opened it ever so slowly. A quiet, subtle *shissss* gave me hope, but the first sip dashed all expectation in a puckering bouquet of vinegar. I fetched another bottle. Same result. "Well, there's plenty of vinegar for pickles," Chris said cheerfully. I was not amused. One by one I opened each bottle and sniffed it, hoping to find an exception. No such luck.

It was obvious that in some way this batch had become contaminated. At the town library I looked in vain for home brewing books that might tell me what to do. Nothing. In the *Encyclopaedia Britannica*, the seven pages on brewing contained an elaborate history and description of commercial brewing technology, but nothing about home brew.

For the next batch, I cleaned the garbage can with a chlorine bleach solution, then scrubbed it with baking soda solution instead of soap and water, and topped out with a clean water rinse just before brewing. I also used the garbage can cover instead of cheesecloth, reasoning that the more airtight I kept the fermenter, the less chance there'd be for contaminating critters to get in and spoil my beer.

At times I felt as scientific as Lister, Jenner, or Pasteur; at other moments I felt like a complete bumbler. I had told my friends I was brewing my own beer, but whenever they asked for a sample, I said I had none left. I didn't reveal that I had thrown out both batches.

This third batch was my make-or-break effort. If it turned sour again, I would go back to my bees. I let it age for a full month. Then one day, after helping a neighboring farmer hay his fields, I was drenched in sweat and grime. What a fine opportunity to try the brew, I thought. I put two bottles in the freezer and sat down on the stoop with the farmer to talk about the coming deer season.

After ten minutes I retrieved the bottles and casually, if carefully, pried off the caps. There was an inviting hiss. I told him that this was my first "real" effort, neglecting to mention that the others had been total failures. The brew looked clear and it had good foam. It smelled a bit yeasty but, wonder of wonders, it tasted like beer—malty, bitter, and refreshing.

In retrospect, it was probably a typically cidery Blue Ribbon home brew. But I thought it was darned good. And so did my neighbor, at least that's what he said. It reminds me now of our first maple syrup when we ignorantly boiled the sap down to industrial-grade darkness, or the first honey from our hives, laced with bits of bee bodies. The beer would win no prizes, but it was drinkable and ours. The emotional investment blotted out a host of faults.

The farmer finished the whole bottle, sediment and all. I drank another bottle. It wasn't exactly smooth, but the flavor was strong and, I thought, very European.

During the next few days I found numerous opportunities to tell friends about my brewing success. In fact, I was about as shy and retiring as a new father. A couple of weeks later, a writer/farmer friend, Nat Tripp, invited us for dinner and suggested, "Since your beer is so good, why not bring some?"

On the night of the party, I chilled a six-pack in the freezer and then wrapped the bottles in an old blanket for the drive over the dirt roads so we wouldn't get hurt if any exploded.

While the other guests helped themselves to gin and tonics or Budweisers, I opened a couple of my bottles. I poured out several glasses and carried them to the guests. The head disappeared in the first twenty seconds, but Nat sniffed appreciatively. "Ah, there's no smell quite like that of home brew!"

Looking like royal servants tasting for poison, two other guests sipped the beer. They paused, their faces stiff masks of politeness. "A little young?" one queried between clenched teeth. "Five weeks," I replied. "Perhaps it needs to age a bit more." The other guinea pig said, "It's okay for home brew," and set the glass down, never to touch it again. One lawyer friend didn't mince words: "You don't mean you prefer this to Bud?"

I laughed, but inside I was hurt. I felt as if I had just helped an elderly lady across the street and instead of thanking me she had kicked me in the shins. I drank the rest of the six-pack myself.

A week or so later, a letter arrived from Tripp. Inside was an article about home brewing from that back-to-the-land missal, *Mother Earth News.*

The article began with a rather mystifying editor's note:

The Justice Department of the Federal Government long ago announced that it would pursue a hands-off policy on any beer made for home consumption and not for sale. In recent years, however, the Alcohol and Tobacco Tax Division of the Treasury Department has informally attempted to enforce commercial laws on home brewers and, thereby, discourage another time-honored, down home, do-it-yourself activity.

Lawyers say the Feds' argument would never hold up in court. Nevertheless, we do not encourage anyone to brew any beer until he is thoroughly satisfied that such activities are completely within the law and that he has complied with all applicable federal, state and local regulations.

Perhaps the editors wanted to cover their rears so the ATF (Alcohol, Tobacco, and Firearms) agents would not swoop down on their office and rummage through their stash of goat's milk and granola bars.

The article itself was decidedly schizophrenic. It delighted in accounts of "friends who experimented with ginger, cracked corn or corn meal. The results were no longer beer but a high octaine [sic] mixture similar to mead. Some of these formulas laid out respectable beer drinkers like they were school boys." On the other hand, it did stress the danger of bottling too early and recommended recording recipes so the brewer could repeat the ones he liked and, presumably, avoid repeating the failures.

Mother Earth News tossed me into the first of several briar patches of conflicting or just plain lousy advice and information. Had I a conspiratorial turn of mind, I might have believed that the writers of this and other articles were ATF agents spreading black propaganda or disinformation about the home brewing craft as a means of suppressing it.

To its credit, the article did help me produce drinkable beer about one time out of three. I poked along for a couple of years, making about four batches a year, knowing I could drink the results even if my friends opted for Bud and Molson. Many bottles did taste like overfermented cider. When I noticed that guests tended to leave glasses of the beer untouched under chairs or to nourish the ferns with it, I realized that home brew was not for everyone. Brewing on this level was like a low-grade addiction: I couldn't give it up, but it didn't incapacitate me.

In 1975, I worked for a newspaper across the Connecticut River in New Hampshire. It was at least a forty-five-minute drive home even on good nights, and in snow it could take twice that long. I confess that I drank two bottles of home brew on that drive every night—one to get to the river and one to get home from there. On particularly hot and thirsty summer evenings, I would buy one of those huge twenty-six-ounce cans of Foster's lager, which look more like oil cans than containers to hold beer.

I learned that there were more sophisticated ways to brew when I found an elementary text in a secondhand bookstore in Boston. *Home Brewing Without Failures,* by H. E. Bravery, made interesting reading but was almost useless for any practical brewing. He called for ingredients unobtainable in the U.S., like Demerara sugar and roasted malt. What's more, his recipes required such procedures as immersing a heater in the grain and water for eight hours. I just wanted to make beer, not start a brewery.

The New Hampshire newspaper folded in 1976, and Chris and I moved so I could take a job in Grand Rapids, Michigan. Grand Rapids remains in my memory a city dominated by the automobile, churches, and beer. We rented half a house across from a Dutch Reformed church that held services in English at 10:00 a.m. and in Dutch at 2:00 p.m. Our landlord next door warned us that people in Grand Rapids took the Sabbath seriously and asked us not to wash the car or mow the grass on Sunday. In his own family, even the "work" of cooking was not done on Sunday.

For most of that year, I was a night police reporter covering fires, highway fatalities, murders, and lesser crimes. When I went out to drink beer with my fellow reporters, I found myself more conscious of their drinking habits. Most of them consumed great quantities of "Fire-Brewed Bohemian Style" Stroh's. On all occasions, drinking was characterized by a race to fill the table with empty bottles and tell stories of past drinking bouts and hangovers. The bars seemed full of boisterous yet lonely people. To them beer was simply a means for getting drunk; not a drink to be savored for its taste. I didn't think of myself as some effete Eastern drinker merely recoiling from the butter-and-eggs boozers of the Midwest. I was sure it was the memory of my struggles to make decent home brew which alienated me from these drinking bouts.

Returning one evening from covering some mayhem, I drove by a store called the Village Wine Cellar, which sold home wine- and beer-making supplies. I went back the following day, and from the moment I entered that room, redolent with the odors of hops, malt, and wine concentrates, my life and beer were never the same.

The proprietor, with the preoccupied air of an academic researcher, introduced himself as Tallmadge Nichols and invited me to browse. One side of the room was devoted to winemaking supplies—grape-crushing tubs, racking equipment, corking devices, cans of fruit concentrate, etc., all displayed under posters of sunny California or France.

It was the other side that caught my fancy: half a store containing home brewing supplies. Back and forth, like a shopper without a list, my eyes roamed from cans of Munton & Fison malt syrup standing like Grenadier Guards, to bags of green- and brown-leaved hops. One shelf held boxes of top-fermenting and bottom-fermenting yeasts. There were bags of hops powders and pellets with exotic names like Bullion, Cascade, and Hallertau. There were small vials of white powders labeled sodium metabisulphite, gypsum, brewing salts, and packets of a brown material that looked like seaweed (and was) but went under the name of Irish Moss. On the floor were large white plastic tubs with tight-fitting lids.

"That's food-grade plastic," Nichols said, breaking into my mental comparison with the green garbage can I used. "Sometimes you can get off-flavors from the other kinds of plastic." Coils of clear plastic hose lay nearby like a whaler's rope. There was a group of glass carboys such as I used to see in office water coolers. Atop each one was a Rube Goldberg device of stiff clear plastic. Near the cash register stood a revolving book rack with manuals and pamphlets about wine- and beermaking.

"I'm in your hands," I told Nichols. "What do I need to make good home brew?"

Nichols led me into the back room. From a refrigerator he drew out a plain brown bottle with a silver cap, and from a shelf he retrieved a long-stemmed beer glass. After carefully opening the bottle, he poured a golden beer into the glass, apologizing that it was only a month old.

That first sip sounded the death knell for my *Mother Earth News* beer. This brew was smooth, bitter without being sour, sweet without being sugary, and well balanced. "How can I make some of this?" I asked. "Very easily," he replied. "We have a standard recipe which we give out to all first-time brewers, and they seem quite satisfied." He added that he didn't generally offer beer to someone off the street, but I seemed to be genuinely interested and not just looking for a free drink.

Nichols had started the store about ten years earlier and first concentrated on winemaking equipment. Home brewing was then limited to Blue Ribbon malt extracts. Its technical illegality and the power of commercial beer advertising had effectively deterred manufacturers from offering a variety of home brewing products for the American market.

In the early 1970s, when British malt manufacturers began to ship their products across the Atlantic, Nichols was one of the first retailers willing to stock them. Along with the ingredients came books by Englishmen such as Dave Line's *Big Book of Brewing*, C. J. Berry's *Home Brewed Beers and Stouts,* and Ken Shales's *Advanced Home Brewing.* The language and measurements were British and a bit confusing. Then the maltmakers began to offer home brew kits with all the ingredients for a batch at a package price. "That changed the market," Nichols observed. "What's more, they provided much better recipes and advice than had existed before."

I told Nichols how faulty I thought the *Mother Earth News* recipe was. Nichols, a man obviously not given to hyperbole, agreed it was "exceedingly bad."

"Most of my customers are more price conscious than quality conscious. They want it simple and easy and cheap. They don't want to make a lot of measurements." On the other hand, heavy beer drinkers did not patronize Nichols's store because "a man who consumes one or two six-packs a night would go through a batch of home brew in less than a week. Such people don't want to spend all their spare time brewing and bottling. In fact, those who make their own beer probably end up drinking less than when they buy it because they have put some of themselves into the brewing."

The few customers who learned their brewing during Prohibition were convinced that nothing could improve their beer. They scorned the English malts as expensive and effete.

"Prohibition-style brewers never spend much time or take temperature readings," Nichols went on. "They put the beer in a container and start drinking it in three days whether it is in the bottle or not. They think that is the only way to make beer. They come in and want to argue that their way is the only way. I don't like to argue. Maybe I have converted a few, but if they made it the old way, it is not likely they will change. The commonest converts to home brewing are those who start from scratch, with no previous knowledge or prejudices."

The lager recipe Nichols gave me called for a can of Munton & Fison malt syrup, dextrose or corn sugar, and Hallertau hops pellets, whose aroma he told me was filling the room.

"You will need some more equipment than I presume you own now," he said. "A secondary fermenter, for example. That's what those carboys are for. Beer needs to ferment under completely airless and thus bacteria-free conditions. Good beer needs to be aged. The plastic device on the carboy is a fermentation lock, or bubbler, which allows the carbon dioxide to escape from the beer without admitting any airborne contaminants. You have to keep water in that bubbler," he warned. Several of his customers had neglected this requirement and wondered why their beer spoiled. "And don't boil the darn thing," he added. Another customer in a fit of sterilizing frenzy had done that and the bubbler had melted into strange and unusable contortions.

Nichols's rule of thumb was to leave the beer in the primary plastic bucket for four or five days for the first bloom of fermentation to occur, then transfer it by plastic tube into the clean secondary fermenter where it remained until the bubbles in the airlock came only every ninety seconds. Depending upon the ambient temperature, the aging could take two to four weeks. At that point, he transferred the five gallons back to the (cleaned) primary, added a cup of dextrose dissolved in hot water, and bottled it in a fashion I was familiar with. He had, however, improved upon my procedure of controlling the flow by pinching the end of the plastic tube with my fingers: he sold plastic twist valves, which reduced the mess and saved about a quart of beer.

I tried my first batch the following Sunday. The directions were simple. I mixed the malt, dextrose, and hops and boiled the lot for forty-five minutes. Then I poured the wort into the primary, freshly cleaned with baking soda and hot water, added enough tap water to make five gallons, and sprinkled the powdered yeast on those untroubled waters.

By the middle of the Dutch services that afternoon, the yeast had begun to work, for there was a telltale layer of tiny bubbles forming on the surface. I carried the forty-five pounds of bucket and liquid to the cool basement and let it perk for the next five days, allowing myself one sniff each day. The surface showed an ugly eruption of gray and brown foam, like Bluto's shaving cream. It smelled inviting, sharp, and fresh, and much hoppier than my Vermont home brew. After five days, the foam had receded and I transferred the brew to the carboy. Like an explorer planting the flag, I attached the fermentation lock and dropped a black plastic garbage bag over the carboy to keep out the light.

I then hauled the carboy back up to the dining room and placed it in a corner. For two weeks it sat there, a squat black sentry with a gradually less frequent hiccough: *blup, blup, blup.* By the end of the second week, the bubbles had slowed to one every ninety seconds. With Clorox, hot water, and baking soda, I cleaned out two cases of Stroh's bottles. I made up the priming sugar and poured it into the clean primary fermenter, then transferred the beer from the carboy using a plastic tube. About a quart of yeasty sediment remained on the bottom of the carboy. The bottles I stored in the coolest corner of the basement.

For three weeks I made impatient moves in their direction. None blew up. One night, after covering a train wreck and a homicide, I felt I really deserved a beer. I stuck one in the freezer, sat down, and waited for fifteen minutes.

When I popped the top, there wasn't much foam, but what a taste!— as good as that which Nichols had served me—smooth, good balance of hops and malt, none of that liquid bread or stiff cidery taste of Prohibition pilsner. I was so pleased that I had another bottle at cellar temperature and went to bed luxuriating in my first real success.

In the following months, I brewed several more batches, varying either the malt or the hops, but not both. Each time the beer tasted different but still good. Along the way, I made my first convert, Roger Conner, an environmental lawyer. Working sixty hours a week and rebuilding his house wasn't enough for Roger. He needed more things to do. Carpentry gave him a thirst, so home brewing was a natural adjunct. I gave him Nichols's recipe and lent him the ingredients. Fortunately, he knew how to follow directions and his first effort was as good as my fourth.

I had no success in sharing my home brew with my hard-drinking newspaper friends. They were not interested, and I didn't force them. I kept Stroh's and Pabst on hand for their visits and, I confess, a few bottles for myself. I knew that they and the imports were still better than my beer.

After a year in Grand Rapids, I found a newspaper job back in Vermont. By the time we left, I was making a fair "house" beer. When we packed the U-Haul for the journey home, the carboy, plastic pail, tubes, and capper were as much a part of our belongings as the dictionary, typewriter, and dog.

The Great Grain Wreck

My first Vermont brewing acolytes were two newspaper reporters and a photographer. We started the evening with two six-packs of the Canadian malt liquor Brador, which one reporter had brought back from a trip to Montreal. By the time we had finished boiling the wort for a Grand Rapids lager, we were pretty rowdy. (The wort is the malt-sugar-laden liquid prior to fermentation; if it has been boiled it is called "bitter" wort, as opposed to sweet.) I lost track of the measurements halfway through the brew, but I didn't think it would matter. The next morning I realized that in my alcoholic fog I had forgotten to put in the yeast. That batch was eventually drinkable, but it had an off-taste that was no doubt related to my lack of attention.

As I brewed my batches of Nichols's lager every couple of months, my consumption of commercial beer declined steadily, although, like a vegetarian who sneaks hamburgers, I would regress on occasion. For several years I didn't force my beer on anyone. Twice burned, thrice shy of offending others. Even when a few people asked for it, I was a master of self-deprecation: "This isn't for everyone," I would warn. Or, "Like the moonshiner said, the only thing I guarantee is that you don't go blind."

But gradually the balance shifted more in favor of my own brew. Chris would drink three or four bottles a week, and an occasional friend might enjoy a glass. When we brought some to a party, a few guests would try it. I drank at least one bottle a night. This meant that the two-case batches were being consumed at a much faster rate than before, like snow melting on a warm spring day.

I had three options: cut down on my consumption, buy more commercial beer, or make larger amounts of my own. I chose the third alternative.

Two obstacles presented themselves. The first was that Burlington water tasted funny. The municipal water system was antiquated, having remained unchanged for seventy years. The water department was about to present a multimillion-dollar bond issue to the voters, but even if approved, repairs would not be completed for four years. To compensate for the failing mechanical and piping system, the city dumped more and more chlorine and other chemicals into the water until it seemed as if you were brushing your teeth in a public swimming pool.

I needed better water. I started carrying empty gallon milk or cider jugs in the trunk of our car, and whenever we visited friends in the country I filled up with their water. This meant that I rarely used water with the same chemical balance twice, but that inconsistency didn't seem to matter in the long run.

The second obstacle was that even as I perfected my technique for Grand Rapids lager and adopted it as my steady brew, I felt twinges of boredom. I began to thirst for some ale and stout, and some different tasting lagers. One day as I was looking through our bookshelves for something to read, I found the three home brewing booklets I had bought in Grand Rapids but had never opened. I chose Byron Burch's *Guide for the Home Production of Fine Beers*.

Burch's book opened with two recipes for a light-bodied pale ale and a dark beer. They seemed pretty complex and involved. There were "flavoring" hops and "aromatic" hops added at different times. The recipe also called for citric acid, gypsum, non-iodized salt, and yeast food.

"If you're a beginner reading this for the first time," Burch wrote, "you're probably bewildered by now by the mass of unfamiliar terms swarming about your head. Don't panic, though, because explanations are coming up, starting here." He was as good as his word. He wrote clearly and well about plastic fermenters, thermometers, and hydrometers, why and how the last are calibrated. Echoing Nichols, Burch recommended food-grade plastic, not cheap garbage cans or crocks. Along the way, he offered good advice, suggesting the home brewer should always clean a new primary fermenter with bicarbonate of soda to neutralize any solvents that might be left over from the manufacturing process. He also described the advantages of cheesecloth and secondary fermenters.

In the "Ingredients" section, Burch discussed different kinds of malt (pale malted barley, crystal or caramel malt, black patent malt, Munich malt) and various sugars (dextrose, sucrose, lactose, brown sugar). He devoted three pages to hops, including "flavoring" hops and "aromatic" hops, and explained the difference between leaf hops, hops pellets, and hops extracts. Since Nichols's recipe called for Hallertau hops, I had not looked further because I was perfectly happy with them at the time, but Burch described hops with evocative names like Pride of Ringwood, Talisman, Brewer's Gold, Cluster, and Northern Brewer. He classified them objectively according to their relative bitterness, and subjectively according to their aroma.

I also learned more about yeast, that marvelous, mysterious, single-celled creature that is the sine qua non of baking and brewing. I came to understand the distinction between the top-fermenting strain used for ales and the bottom-fermenting variety common to lagers.

Baker's yeast does work for beer, but it has several major drawbacks, Burch said. It reproduces best at higher temperatures, where the threat of infection is much greater; it doesn't settle well, and thus home brew made with it is always cloudy. Finally, it was developed to create the maximum amount of carbon dioxide to make bread rise. Now I understand why my early beers tasted so yeasty.

Under "Optional Equipment," Burch listed items like a bottle-washer sprayer that could be attached to a kitchen faucet, hose clamps to aid in bottling, and an office scale for measuring small amounts of hops. Other items were familiar—good, solid, returnable green or dark brown bottles and a strong capper. I felt like a pioneer, long in the woods, who happens upon a general store.

When I finished the book, I thought ruefully how helpful it would have been five years earlier when I started brewing. But it hadn't been available then. Fortunately, I didn't have to look far to find some of the supplies he wrote about. Garden Way Living Center, a division of the Garden Way companies devoted to self-sufficient living, had several shelves of home wine- and beermaking paraphernalia.

However, for all of its selection, the store did not carry any of the flavoring hops varieties Burch recommended for his light-bodied pale ale. All it offered was Fuggles, Cascades (which Burch recommended for aromatic hops), and my old workhorse, Hallertau. On the spot I formulated a rule of thumb for the home brewer: be flexible. Never be afraid to substitute and create your own recipes, because no home brew store is ever likely to carry all the exact ingredients required for any but the most elementary of recipes.

The major purchase from Garden Way was my first hydrometer. Burch thought it indispensable. As a "brewer's compass," it allows you to measure the progressive conversion of sugars into alcohol and carbon dioxide. The hydrometer calculates the specific gravity or weight of the liquid. Sugar dissolved in water is denser or heavier than plain water, while alcohol is lighter. As the yeast converts sugars, the density of the solution falls and thus the hydrometer will sink lower in the solution. The scale inside the instrument shows the potential alcohol when you start so you can accurately predict what the final alcoholic content will be.

One hard-to-solve problem is that hydrometers seldom agree with each other. Just stick to one that seems to be consistent.

Burch explained that the higher the ratio of malt sugars to corn sugars, the higher the final gravity will be because malt sugars are not refined enough to convert completely. Some of their solids always remain in solution and keep the final gravity above 1000. While Burch made this explanation clear and concise, another home brew book quite blithely ordered the brewer to bottle only when gravity reached zero. Once a friend of mine left a batch in the secondary for three months waiting for it to reach that impossible figure.

The best ingredients and recipes are only as good as the containers in which the brewing occurs. Cleanliness here is as close to goodness as it is to godliness. Thanks again to Burch, I learned about the marvels of bleach and sodium metabisulphite. Chlorine bleach is an excellent sterilizer and cleanser when used carefully and rinsed out thoroughly. If bleach is followed by a rinse of sodium metabisulphite, the vessels and bottles will have no residual film or aftertaste and should be clean enough to thwart all infection. Conversely, I finally understood that soap and detergents are anathema to good beer because of the film they leave behind. That is why many bars don't use soap on their beer glasses—soap and detergent kill the head. The head may be extraneous to the taste, but beer without a head looks more like ginger ale than beer.

When I turned to the other brewing books, I was glad I had read Burch first. They were inferior volumes of oversimplification and outright error. One called itself a "complete" guide to home brewing but turned out to be nothing more than a marketing device for the author's products. It asserted, for example, that "Years of experimenting with the various yeast strains has established that the _____ brand [the brand he happened to sell] is the best yeast for all beers, including stout."

In the next year, I made six or eight batches from Burch's book: pale ales, brown ales, lagers, and a "steam beer." I experimented with adding small amounts of salt, gypsum, citric acid, and gelatin to clear the beer. I really couldn't tell if these ingredients helped the taste, but they made me feel more professional.

Overall, Burch's beers were noticeably better than my Grand Rapids lager, although the difference between them was not as great as between Grand Rapids and the original Blue Ribbon brew. I loved to experiment with different ratios of malt to hops in the hope I could approximate some of the great beers of the world like Guinness or Spatenbräu. That I didn't come close didn't matter.

Home brew began to find a niche as a liquid "thank you." It became an offering of something more personal than money or words. I have given beer to the town employee who graded our dirt road in St. Johnsbury. I have used it to thank the plumber for fixing our furnace on a wild wintry night. The manager of the restaurant supply store where I buy brewing equipment earned a bottle for his help in finding a stainless steel pot. When we burden the garbage man with extra debris, he gets a home brew. The stereo repairman who fixed a receiver free of charge won a six-pack of porter.

Exchanging beer for services probably placed me in the underground economy and thanks to bartering, I made another convert. Professor Peter Seybolt is a man of many parts—a good tennis player, fly-fisherman, and pig farmer as well as a teacher of Chinese history. In his farming capacity, Peter asked us to trade some of our labor for some of his spiced sausage. I brought a six-pack of home brew to drink as we ground and packed the slippery meat. Then we invited him to help us bottle a batch in return for more home brew. As we bottled, he became so intrigued that he went to Garden Way and bought all the necessary equipment.

My reputation as a home brewer began to spread like the smell of French fries out of a diner's ventilator. This was literally and figuratively so, for when I brewed a batch and turned on the exhaust fan above the stove, one could smell the Mares brewery three houses away.

One evening, during a conversation with friends who owned a small construction company, I learned they had registered the name Lake Champlain Monster Brewing Company with the Secretary of State. The name referred to the local version of the much-sought denizen of Loch Ness. That summer there was a flurry of "sightings" of the monster. A minor tourist attraction was born. Although they were not brewers, these friends were hearty beer drinkers who dreamed of a combination saloon and brewery that would dispense Monster Beer to students and tourists. I was intrigued enough by the idea to suggest an intermediate step—put a notice in the paper to solicit interest in a home brewing club. I thought these future commercial brewers ought to have some practical experience.

The organizational meeting of the Vermont Home Brewers Association took place at the construction company's warehouse one warm August evening. Each person was to bring a six-pack or its equivalent of his favorite beer. I was the only one to bring home brew. The others provided the likes of Fischer's, Guinness, Beck's, and Moosehead.

I knew all seven people present except Barton Merle-Smith, late of Boulder, Colorado, and now the owner of Barton's Hot Tubs in Burlington. Barton's ample midsection was covered by a stained T-shirt emblazoned with an emblem of the American Homebrewers Association: a smiling turkey clasping sheaves of barley in one foot and an overflowing bottle of home brew in the other.

It was soon apparent that Barton knew a lot more about home brew than I did. For an hour he regaled us with stories about brewing in Boulder and the American Homebrewers Association. The AHA, we learned, was founded early in the 1970s by a nuclear engineering dropout and alternative school teacher named Charlie Papazian. He began teaching home brewing for a little extra cash and launched the organization out of a spare room in his house. He applied for and received tax-exempt status from the Internal Revenue Service, which made contributions tax-deductible. Here was a philanthropic organization dedicated to spreading the gospel of home brew. Barton passed around Papazian's own text, *The New Joy of Home Brewing*, and copies of the AHA magazine, *Zymurgy*, the only magazine I've ever seen that defines its title on the cover. "Zymurgy: dealing with the fermentation process, as in brewing." The motto of the AHA is "Relax. Don't Worry. Have a Homebrew!" When I later sent them $50, I became a Diamond-Studded Platinum Mug Sponsor with a membership card which expired "Never."

Barton's first brew was called Long Distance Lager because he had made it according to directions from his brother in Boulder during a two-hour telephone call. Like a film dissolve, that story merged into his description of a "beer and steer," where a whole cow was roasted, the guests consumed five or ten kegs of home brew, and then jumped naked into a bank of hot tubs.

Zymurgy was full of good information, book reviews, discussions of technique, and accounts of local and national home brewing contests. There were recipes with names like Danger Knows No Favorites Dark Lager, Goat Scrotum Ale, and Whitey's No-Show Ale. Sprinkled throughout its well-illustrated pages were anecdotes and one-liners. Stealing from Fat Freddy of the Fabulous Furry Freak Brothers comics, one wag paraphrased, "Home brew will get you through times of no money better than money will get you through times of no home brew."

P. T. Davis of Seattle captured the spirit of home brewing when he wrote in the Letters column: "I survived Mt. St. Helens, although not by much—drank too much home brew Saturday night, May 17, and overslept, thus did not arrive at Spirit Lake in time for my demise. Relax and have a home brew. It saves lives from volcanoes and no doubt from other disasters as well."

Even the club notes brought chuckles for some of the names. Besides the Maltose Falcons and San Andreas Malts, there were the Mile-high Masterspargers, Redwood Lagers, San Gabriel Valley Wort Hogs, and the Christian Ferment League at Princeton Theological Seminary in New Jersey.

Zymurgy introduced me to a whole subculture of home brewers. These were not people who just poured more sugar into the brew to give it a bigger alcohol boost. Nor were they old-line, stalwart home brewers who were satisfied with Blue Ribbon malt. Brewing was part of their lives, just like buying coffee or planting peas in the spring. They formed a collection of serious beermaking cranks, technocrats, and mavericks who still valued the fences of good recipes and directions. They were restless experimenters who enjoyed what one called their "mud-pies-for-adults" activity.

I reported on my eighteen-month campaign to have a home brew contest at the Champlain Valley Exposition, the state's largest fair. The year before, I had tried to interest fair officials in such a contest. I argued that home brewing was an ancient and honorable craft, which gave its practitioners as much pride and demanded as much skill as the making of quilts and apple pies. Furthermore, President Jimmy Carter had just signed the bill that permitted the manufacture of up to two hundred gallons of home brew per household. What better way to spread the word than to have a home brew contest? The clinching argument, I thought, was that the home brew law specifically allowed its transportation to public places for the purpose of judgings and tastings.

The fair manager listened politely, but explained that six weeks was not enough time to get directors' approval and insert a new category in the program of prizes. He suggested that I resubmit the proposal the following year.

The week after the club meeting, Barton, who had been elected president, and I put on clean shirts, packed two bottles of home brew in a briefcase, and went to see the manager. He told us he had already recommended that the contest be allowed. The fair board of directors had given its approval, provided it was legal. That meant they wanted to ask the Liquor Control Board, which oversees all distribution of alcohol in the state. I thought we were home free. The fair already had a beer sales tent. We were only proposing that home brew be sipped by four judges. None would be sold, and none would be given away.

Just to be on the safe side, a lawyer friend and I went before the Liquor Control Board's monthly meeting to repeat our request. We were greeted with a few hearty jokes but no decision. The board felt it should submit the question to the state attorney general. All this buck-passing made me nervous, but I still believed that no open-minded person could quash such an innocent activity. After all, the board was in the business of peddling hard liquor to the Vermont public.

Alas, we had not plumbed the depths of caution of that body and of an assistant attorney general who recommended denial on the basis of a Catch-22 statute which said in effect, "Thou shalt not do anything except as provided in this law." Their interpretation was that our contest amounted to free distribution and consumption of beer and was therefore illegal.

Outraged, I went to the county state's attorney and persuaded him to write a letter to fair officials saying that if such a contest were held, he would not prosecute because he had "more important things to do." The authorities remained unmoved.

(A year later I saw a member of the Liquor Control Board on the street and asked if we would ever be allowed to have our contest. He lowered his voice, winked, and said, "Just don't ask next time.")

The Burlington *Free Press* tried to mediate editorially, suggesting that we ask for a license to *sell* the beer, the better to comply with the law. "It's just possible that what the Vermont Home Brewers Association could not give away might be all right if they charge a fee." I was intrigued with the idea, but so annoyed at the mixture of narrow interpretation and timidity along the line that I didn't pursue it.

A few days later I received a call from Steve Morris of the Cram Hill Brewers Association, the only other home brew club in Vermont. I had heard about these ten or fifteen people, most of whom worked at Vermont Castings stove company in the town of Randolph. They were so well organized that they even had a club song. It purposely didn't have any words so the members couldn't forget them. Morris had been quoted in *Zymurgy* as saying, "The American beer drinker has less variety available to him than any other beer drinker in the world. Cram Hill Brewers Association tries to promote organically pure, tasty beer and lots of varieties." Having read of our tribulations with the Liquor Control Board, he generously offered, "Let's have the contest at my house. We have an annual eight-mile road race, the West Brookfield Classic, and a sheep roast on Labor Day. We won't make a big deal of it, just invite the people we know. It would be great to add a home brew contest to the celebration."

By the time he hung up, I had agreed to rally all the home brewers I knew and take their entries down to West Brookfield (pop. 50). If brewers wanted to come in person, so much the merrier. We thought that fifteen entries would mean success and twenty-five would make a "happening." Cram Hill members would provide the storage, ice, judging paraphernalia, and prizes. Publicity we would not seek. I was amused at the thought of state police raiding the contest and breaking all our bottles. After a few beers we would have no trouble "going limp" to passively protest our right to taste, judge, and drink home brew in public. As a precaution, we took along an attorney, ostensibly to watch his son run in the race, but with the secret plan that he would represent us if the police swept in to enforce that ridiculous law.

Labor Day that year was one of those muggy, dog days that remind Vermonters how lucky they are not to live farther south. The hamlet of West Brookfield consists of about ten houses sprinkled around a tiny church and a converted one-room schoolhouse. Steep hills slope up both sides of a mile-long valley, whose two hundred acres belong to a single dairy farm. Sheep graze on the hillsides, and on this day smoke was rising from Morris's barbecue pit where two of their fellows were roasting.

I stowed the case of assorted entries from Burlington and took my place at the starting line for the eight-mile race. At 10:00 a.m. sharp, thirty runners started off from under a makeshift banner stretched between two dead elms. It was a tough race, four miles straight up the valley to drain the lungs and four miles straight down to pulverize the knees and Achilles tendons. Steve Morris and I ran as twins to finish in a dripping, respectable fifty-seven minutes.

We were ready for beer. Twenty-two people had provided twenty-eight entries. We picked judges on the spot, the only proviso being that none could pass judgment on his own beer.

Morris had printed up some slips of paper with sought-for criteria: head, aroma, taste, aftertaste. We made up the rules and a scoring system as we went along. Our five categories were light ale, dark ale, lager, stout, and Sleazo. The last honored Cram Hill brewer Stanley

Leon, who, through many years of lonely and difficult labor, had perfected an infamous local concoction named Stanley's Sleazo. Local wags defined it as "the mostest with the leastest." By definition, the Sleazo category contained anything the brewer desired as long as he was committed to the cheapest possible ingredients and the fastest brewing time. Usually this meant Blue Ribbon malt as a base, then whatever sugars were around (cane, molasses, honey, or maple syrup), baker's yeast, and any flavoring from ginger root to vanilla extract. The beer would sit for perhaps three to four days in a single fermenter and then go into containers; these could be screw-top bottles, plastic cider jugs, or whatever was available. If ever there was a beer designed to recall the explosive effervescence of Prohibition, this was it.

I think we started with twelve judges. There seemed to be a strong inverse relationship between the desire to judge and brewing experience. We tried to give the novices a quick course in bitterness versus sourness, malt flavor versus cider, and sipping versus slurping. But within fifteen minutes the judging had become pretty free-form ... and free-foam. At least a third of the bottles were so overprimed that they spewed their contents over judges, notebooks, and observers indiscriminately. One of these beers was actually named Stand Back Lager.

As the afternoon wore on and the novelty wore off, some of the fair-weather judges passed their pencils to unsuspecting friends and slunk off to eat lamb, drink commercial beer, and play volleyball.

Unquestionably, the toughest category was Sleazo. I know because I judged it. Some of those entries were, as H. L. Mencken once said of President Harding's prose, "so awful that a certain grandeur crept in." One tasted simply like vinegar. Another reeked of apple cider gone bad. I sprayed my chest with the contents of one entry. Another produced so much foam that I never did get a taste. And one was so yeasty I felt I'd been dunked in a vat of sourdough. With each sip, I dreaded the next entry more.

The balm for the worst hangover in many years was my victory in the stout category. Peter Seybolt won the lager class with his first-ever batch. The prizes included a modern Stroh's beer tray, a case of old glass bottles, an American Homebrewers Association T-shirt, and one of the first beer cans ever made (1934) from Kreuger Ale in Vir-

ginia. Steve Morris had found a case of these cans in an abandoned garage. Printed on the can were instructions on how to use an opener. Since we got to choose our prizes, I picked the can. I later found out that to collectors it is worth over $100.

Last and (very much) least, Charlie Page of Randolph, a man whose style of beermaking a friend described as "turning over rocks to find something interesting to add to the beer," won a bottle of Ripple for his winning Sleazo entry.

A week later, a local television reporter called me to ask if he could tape a short segment about home brewing. He brought his electronic entourage of video, lights, microphones, and fixed questions: How often does a bottle blow up? How strong is the beer? Are you worried about raids from ATF agents? Dressed in American Homebrewers Association T-shirts, Barton Merle-Smith and I demonstrated our equipment in my kitchen. The camera made a sweep of the shelf holding over seventy-five different bottles and cans of imported and better domestic beers (including the Kreuger can), which made the room look like a college dormitory.

I fantasized that a two-minute spot on television would recruit platoons of home brewers to help free the innocent from subjection to Big Brewer. Like any social climber, I didn't hesitate to drop my new title, Vermont State Stout Champion, at the slightest opportunity. At the same time I felt again those itches of boredom, which I had noticed after mastering Grand Rapids lager. I was like the novice sky-diver who tires of static line jumps as he dreams of free-fall. The more I read *Zymurgy* and *Amateur Brewer* (an advanced home brewing newsletter from Portland, Oregon), the more I was convinced that first-class brewing went far beyond malt extracts and hops pellets.

To reach that special state of grace and accomplishment, I had to enter the world of "all-grain brewing." It required learning techniques I had only read about, like mashing, sparging, and water treatment. I had never seen anyone actually make all-grain beer, as it is called. My beers were all-malt because I used no rice, wheat, or other substitutes. But "all-grain" for advanced brewers means grinding the malted barley, mashing it, and straining out the sugars (sparging), all to get to the point where an extract brewer opens a can of malt syrup or a bag of powdered malt.

Since leaving Grand Rapids and Nichols's store, I had made a habit of visiting home brewing suppliers wherever I found them. One of those was Winemakers Supplies in Northampton, Massachusetts, owned by Frank Romanowski.

Romanowski had been a baker who, fifteen years earlier, began making his own wine. This led him to stocking and selling home wine-making supplies. In a few years, the winemaking business exceeded that of the bakery. He sold the latter and expanded his wares to include beermaking supplies. At the same time, he started brewing himself. Whereas Nichols's customers were primarily interested in the simplest and most reliable ingredients and recipes, Romanowski encouraged his customers to experiment. His store was a bit smaller than Nichols's, but it seemed to have both more equipment and a greater variety of ingredients: six kinds of hops, for example. Romanowski and his wife ran the business with the help of George Peppard, who had worked for four months at an English brewery and had dreams of opening his own place in nearby Easthampton.

On my second trip to Northampton, Romanowski offered some of his own pale ale. It was superb—smooth, mellow, and as good as any English bitter I had ever drunk. "This is all-grain beer," he said. "No matter how hard you try, you simply cannot duplicate this with extracts because extracts cannot provide enough body." My beer was obviously thinner and more superficial by comparison.

Again, the past was prologue. I *had* to make all-grain beer. Impatient brewer that I am, I didn't bother to question Romanowski about the technique. I assumed the admirable Burch would tell me all about it in his book. I bought twenty pounds of "two-row" barley and declined Romanowski's offer to grind it for an extra 10 cents per pound.

At home, the first task therefore was to grind the barley, but I now realized I had no idea how fine to make it. I remembered reading somewhere about just cracking the husk. In a section on "Mashing for Flavor," Burch recommended grinding grain with a rolling pin, a coffee grinder, or a blender. Five messy minutes with a rolling pin sent me to the coffee grinder. Using its coarsest setting, I finished the job in twenty minutes, and left a fine layer of grain dust on every horizontal surface of the kitchen.

"Relax. Don't worry. Have a homebrew," I said to myself. I moved

on to Burch's one-page section on "Advanced Mashing Techniques."
He said that British books on the subject were misleading for Americans because British malts are more "modified," or converted to fermentable sugars. "With American grain malts," he warned, "you must
go through some additional steps not necessary with their British
counterparts. The mash is first raised to 95–100 degrees F. and held
for one hour. Raise it again to 135 degrees and hold for 20–30 minutes.
Raise it then to 150 degrees and hold for 45–60 minutes. Finally, raise
it to 170 degrees for ten minutes prior to sparging."

For the first time, I realized that this was not going to be easy.
Having already turned the kitchen into a flour mill, I then discovered
that the pot I'd used for my previous batches could not hold more than
half the grains and the accompanying water. This sent me to the
neighbors' for a bigger pot. Burch was unclear about how much water
to use, and I made an executive decision to hold the mess-mash to the
consistency of half-cooked oatmeal. I kept track of the temperature
increases with a candy thermometer.

Four hours later, I finished the boiling portion of Burch's recipe. I
tested for starch with a drop of iodine on several drops of mash water.
The solution turned brown, not blue, which indicated that all the
starches had been converted to sugars. I was ready to sparge, or rinse,
all the sugars off the grains and make the resulting liquid the basis of
the wort. This would become my substitute for the can of malt extract.

Burch told me to "pour off the free liquid." He suggested several
sparging equipment arrangements: a vegetable steamer basket, a camp
cooler, or two plastic pails fitted together, the inner one punched full
of small holes. I opted for the strainer because it was all I had. Meanwhile, I realized I would have to heat five to six gallons of water for
sparging, and again my brew kettle wouldn't be big enough. Like a
beleaguered military commander pressing the cooks and clerks into
service, I recruited our eight-gallon enamel canner. The canner was so
large that it covered two stove burners.

I hung the strainer basket inside the biggest bowl I had. Then,
with a two-quart saucepan, I ladled the grains into the strainer and
sprinkled some of my 160-degree water from the canner over them.
One quart of water for one quart of grains seemed reasonable. I tossed
the spent grains into a bucket for later deposit on the compost heap.

The sparging operation lasted at least an hour. When I had collected a total of five and a half gallons of potato-colored water, I poured it back into the canner, added the first charge of hops, and turned up the heat. Waiting for it to boil gave me time to clean up the floor, extra pots and pans, spoons, ladles, and other brewing debris.

Just as I was finishing the mop-up and on my way to the basement with some pans, I heard a hiss of liquid striking fire. I rushed up the steps to see a greenish slime snaking out from under the canner lid and down the side. One burner was already extinguished, and the air was thick with the smell of burnt sugar. I turned off the second burner to assess the damage. It took me fifteen minutes to clean up the sticky mess. In twenty batches of beer, this was the first boilover I had experienced. I swore it would be the last. Thirty minutes later I finished the boil, turned off the heat, and added the aromatic hops.

I scooped out a half-pint of wort and placed it in the refrigerator freezer to cool so I could take a hydrometer reading. Then I carried the entire canner to the basement and put it outside in subfreezing temperatures to cool.

It was time to test the original gravity. Two different kinds of degrees here make for confusion. Degrees of extract measure the amount of sugars extracted from the malt or corn sugar and now contained in solution. The hydrometer gives you the density or gravity of the liquid. It is calibrated to read correctly at 60° F. (All new hydrometers contain a chart listing corrections for temperature variations.)

Burch wrote that pale malted barley should give roughly twenty-four gravity degrees per pound of grain. I had ten pounds. Ten times twenty-four equals two-forty, divided by five eventual gallons of beer, would give me an original gravity of 1048, *IF* I had done everything according to Hoyle.

I cooled a cup of wort to 60° F. by placing it in the deep freeze. Then I poured the contents into the hydrometer's plastic tube. I shook the liquid to get rid of the bubbles and peered at the meniscus. It read . . . 1024. I shook the instrument again and rubbed my eyes. It was still 1024. That was 15 degrees below even my lowest estimate. I was deeply disappointed. No, I was angry, at Fate, at myself. It made little difference. To spend ten hours, create havoc in the kitchen and have such thin beer for my pain, was mortifying.

No matter how low the reading, I was damned if I would throw out that batch of beer. I scooped out a gallon of the still steaming wort, added two pounds of dried malt extract, dissolved it well, boiled it for ten minutes, and poured it back into the primary fermenter. That brought the number of extract degrees to about 1038 or 1040. I knew I was cheating, but how else could I save it?

The next morning the temperature of the wort had dropped to 80° F. and I added two packets of yeast. Six hours later, fermentation had begun.

During the next few weeks, I thought about that day's work. What conceivable economic, aesthetic, social, culinary, or egoistic benefit could possibly derive from so much messy labor?

At first I wanted to blame Burch. Why hadn't he given more space to the complexities of mashing, made his language clearer, told his readers they would be joining a religious order, not just making a confession? To be fair, his book was for the average novice brewer. When I reread the "Advanced Mashing Techniques" section, I saw it was only meant to be an outline, not a recipe or detailed description. I then realized that mashing is a complex and time-consuming procedure and that I would have to seek advice elsewhere.

When I tasted my first mashed ale some six weeks later, it did have a bit more body and smoothness than my extracts, but it also had two pounds of dried malt extract that weren't supposed to be there. There was certainly no hint of greatness.

I added up the pros and cons of sticking to extracts. Romanowski's all-grain beer was 75 to 100 percent better than any extract I had ever made, and it seemed likely that my mashing-sparging technique could be improved with better equipment. I thought I should be able to cut the time from ten hours to seven, or three times what an extract brew required. Was it worth it?

I determined to be more efficient and shorten the brewing time before answering that question.

Who Brews?

In the summer of 1981, while leafing through a copy of *The New Republic* in search of liberal answers to the world's problems, I came upon Nicholas von Hoffman's column about stocks, "Nick's Picks." In this article, he expatiated on the marvelous "up-side potential" of several beer company stocks, especially Anheuser-Busch.

Von Hoffman's praise annoyed me sufficiently to take pen in hand for a rejoinder. I wrote:

> With respect to "A Fool and His Money: Slots and Suds" by Nicholas von Hoffman (*TNR*, June 20), I plead guilty to von Hoffman's label of a "downcast liberal who doesn't believe in Reaganomics," but there he and I part company, at least on the subject of beer stocks.
>
> At the cost of a single share of Anheuser-Busch stock [selling then at $35], von Hoffman could buy the basic paraphernalia and ingredients to make, bottle, and cap two cases of his own beer or ale. In less than six weeks, his beer/ale would rise spectacularly (in quality) while Bud, Schlitz, and Miller would remain unchanged.
>
> Why are people in rural Vermont paying $4.50 a six-pack for Moosehead from Canada, Foster's from Australia, or even Heineken? It's because, as Mike Royko once suggested, "Most American beer tastes as if it had been brewed through a horse."
>
> It costs me about $11 to brew two cases of excellent lager, ale, or stout. It would take more than Clydesdales to drag me back to

that bland, tasteless liquid that passes for most commercial beer in this country.

Two weeks later the letter appeared on the correspondence page of *TNR* under the subheading "A Better Brew." I was pleased and surprised when, over the next several weeks, I received three phone calls and seven letters from readers across the country—New York, Massachusetts, Georgia, Washington, Arizona, Texas. Several were already home brewers and just wrote to say "Amen." Others wanted me to help them get started with the "quality-enhancing potential of home brewing," as one woman wrote. A man from Massachusetts agreed that "a good beer is hard to come by. What can I do about it?"

Whenever the correspondents asked for information, I suggested a couple of books and a subscription to *Zymurgy*. I was fascinated that this simple letter, penned in humor and ill-humor, had aroused such interest in a political and literary journal. If these readers were excited, what about people who regularly drank imported beers, or college students, or good cooks generally? Might they also become converts?

Who are the home brewers of this world? A random sample from our club in Burlington includes: Dieter Gump, M.D.; Geoffrey Burnham, calligrapher; Hal Boutelier, art supplies dealer; William Lipke, art historian; Ralph Swenson, college administrator; Doug French, goldsmith; Dennis Kauppila, agricultural extension agent; Mike Richardson, community organizer; Dick Heilman and Bernie Saks, radiologists; Jack Long, pediatrician; Peter Seybolt, professor of Chinese history; Hank Kite, social worker; Barton Merle-Smith, hot tubs entrepreneur; Peter Bergh, architect.

What makes them different from the rest of the beer drinkers? They are almost all professionals, people who have enough money to drink imported beer if they choose. They are discriminating, not heavy drinkers. Their educated taste buds come from travels abroad, from curiosity about the imports on the shelves, or from dissatisfaction with largely undifferentiated American beers.

There is no single reason why people brew their own beer, any more than there is a single reason why people fly ultralight aircraft, collect Depression glass, or raise show dogs. Some of the reasons for joining the Vermont Home Brewers Association were the superior taste of home brew, the attraction of pure, natural ingredients, the desire for revenge against major brewers, the fun of experimentation, and the pride in doing something for oneself.

The most common reason for making home brew is a genuine taste and love for good beer which is not being satisfied by the commercial brands. Home brewers are simultaneously angry about the vapid, homogenized taste of most American beers and distressed by the high price of imported ones. (Throughout this book, I have used the male pronoun to describe the average home brewer, simply because far more men than women practice this hobby. However, it is certainly not limited to men. In fact, Nancy Vineyard of Santa Rosa, California, won the Homebrewer of the Year Award at the 1983 AHA national championships.)

Another class of home brewers is what writer Fred Eckhardt calls the "cheap beer crowd." Their prime motivation for brewing at home is economic. They may drink a lot, simply have little money, or both. The cheap beer people don't want anything fancy, just simple ingredients and a straightforward recipe they can follow every two or three weeks when the mood or thirst hits them. Boil it, cool it, get the yeast in, ferment it for a few days, and fill those bottles. Age for a couple of weeks and drink it down. The cheap beer crowd probably doesn't try to please anyone except themselves.

Epitomizing the cheap beer crowd were two Germans I once met in a Denver home brew shop. I was talking to the proprietors when the pair entered. "Here come the Katzenjammer Kids," one owner said. They were built like National Football League guards. They wanted two cases of extract syrup—twelve cans. This would provide a month's worth of drinking—six batches, or thirty gallons. The store owners said they came in every month and bought the same thing.

When I asked them why they were brewing at home, they said, "We are German, and we know good beer. To get good German beer here is impossible unless you have much money; therefore we make our own."

This class of beer drinkers may or may not want to boost the alcohol content. Many novice home brewers love to raise the octane of their beer by adding more cheap sugar. Such a practice was widespread during Prohibition, when people were more interested in getting snockered than in brewing fine beer. This subspecies of swaggering, often staggering brewers often embarrass their more serious brethren. They love to brag about their beer with 8 to 10 percent alcohol. Legally this is not beer, but malt liquor, although with the high percentage of nonmalt sugars, it isn't even much of a malt beverage. These brewers don't care; they want to get high.

A third class of home brewers works hard to develop and refine a house brand. They seek a steady supply of beer, rather like a neat pile of firewood or a crop of ripe tomatoes. Once they achieve a certain level of competence, they stick to what is safe and sure.

Once a brewer has his "own" beer, he usually wants a personal label. I asked an artist friend if he would design one in return for some stout. In a week's time I had a thousand of them. The only problem is that it takes hours to soak and scrub off the commercial labels. One solution that works fairly well is to soak the bottles for an hour in two ounces of tri-sodium phosphate per ten gallons of water.

Most brewers desire external recognition to go with internal pride. They like the inner warmth of seeing their bottles standing at hospitable attention on the shelves or in the basement. They devise ways to nudge their guests to try some. They are not above a private marketing campaign on behalf of their brew.

An extreme and, mercifully, small number of home brewers are intensely self-deprecating. These people either publicly deride their own beer or apologize for it at the first hint of criticism. They point out some flaw in the ingredients or process and claim that the "next" batch will be much better. Finally, after you have given up hope that you'll ever taste any of their "decent" beer, they bring one out. You taste it and it's fair. Not great, but certainly not as wretched as they imply. So you tell them so. "Hey, Jake, this isn't so bad." Then if you look closely you are likely to see a small wince of pain or irritation, and you realize that all that self-flagellation was a mere mask for overweening (and often misplaced) pride.

Insecurity is a passing phase for almost all home brewers, but a few never outgrow it. This is the group which lives by the aphorism of La Rochefoucauld: "We confess to little faults only to persuade ourselves that we have no great ones." Someone once said to me, "I don't know which is worse, Mares, when you were good company and your beer was lousy, or now when your beer is good and you talk of nothing else."

In a more perverse manifestation of insecurity, a brewer may serve up bad beer and then dare the drinker not to like it. He is so caught up in his brewing that he cannot distinguish between himself as a human being and his talent as a brewer. He must have both praise and approval. This quirk, of course, is not unique to brewers. Anyone who has spent his weekend on a project only to have it go bad, whether it's the new fence that collapses or the fish that gets away, wants approval for the expended effort.

Most home brewers, however, are anxious to share their brews and skills with others. They have a proselytizing streak. They want to convert the heathen who are still drinking standard American beer. In the gentle words of J. I. Rodale, founder of *Organic Gardening*, speaking of his discovery of composting: "I felt I had to share this experience with the rest of the country. It would not be fair to know this and say nothing about it."

The proselytizing home brewer faces a contradiction. He can't expect to convert the confirmed "light" beer drinker without giving him something that is very close to what he is accustomed to. But if a light beer drinker likes your beer, you might well wonder if it's flavorful enough. There is something to Groucho Marx's famous line, "I wouldn't want to belong to any club which would accept me as a member." If a brew appeals to everyone, it is by nature undistinguished.

The solution is to be guided by your own tastes and preferences. That way, you will have at least one satisfied customer. And if you are devoted to light beer, you probably should not try to brew your own. It will have too much taste for you.

Some home brewers constantly experiment with ingredients or equipment. They know that brewing will always be a mixture of art and technology. Some concentrate on experiments with malts and hops to explore different tastes. Like Paul Angerhofer of the Washington, D.C., brewing club BURP (Brewers United for Real Potables), these people deliberately "never make the same beer twice." After all, the home brewer nowadays has a great range of materials, even without mashing. For the commercial brewer, inconsistency is the work of the devil. For the home brewer, inconsistency (assuming the beer is not infected) is one of the joys.

For other experimenters, the production process is more interesting. Hal Boutelier, one of my mentors, has never stopped experimenting in a dozen years of brewing. He takes one bit of information out of this book, another from that fellow brewer, and writes it all down. He knows the old methods of brewing are too primitive and inexact, so he creates new ones. He is an equipment perfectionist, always searching for a good used refrigerator, a quicker wort chiller, a bigger pot, a better sparging vessel.

Finally, there are those brewers who care strongly about what foods they put into their bodies. Their caution about meat and vegetables extends to their beer. Beer is one of the last classes of food to resist public demand for "natural" ingredients. The brewing industry has steadfastly fought off all attempts to require it to list ingredients on the label. Permissible additives are listed in the *Congressional Record*, but the average drinker has no way of knowing which, if any, of these chemicals are in his beer. A home brewer hears about substances used by commercial brewers, such as propylene glycol alginate, gallo-tannin, sodium reythorbate, and ethyl isobutyrate, and wonders why decent beer should need all those foaming agents, stabilizers, color enhancers, and clarifiers. Home brewers know that if they want a heading agent or a clearing agent, they can use natural substances like gum arabic, licorice, or gelatin.

Finally, brewing, like winemaking, gives you a wonderful feeling of possession and pride when you go down to your cellar or enter your closet to select a beverage for an occasion. These are not drinks made in France or Germany or Canada. These are your own offerings produced in your own kitchen.

How do I know about all these different reasons for brewing? Because at one time or another, I have acutely experienced them all.

The Ingredients

Once again, a choice was at hand. I could stick to my extracts and experiment ad infinitum with different hops and malt syrups or crystal grain and maintain my current production of one batch (two cases) every four to six weeks. In four years I had found or developed three brews—a lager, an ale, and a stout—that I (and most of our guests) liked. My talents were publicly recognized through my victory in the home brew championships. As long as I kept my mouth shut, no one but Chris would know of my all-grain disaster. Brewing two cases of beer made for a long day. If I calculated my time at $5 an hour and the ingredients at $15, all-grain brew would cost roughly $1.80 per bottle. I could drink a lot of Heineken and Guinness for that.

But I was beyond infatuation. I was in love with the seductive aroma and taste of real, mashed beer. Extracts were beginning to bore me. Despite my failure, I knew the taste of real, mashed beer was no mirage. Getting there would just take a bit longer and require more preparations. Also, I realized that I was generally happier wrestling with a new problem than coasting on a past solution.

Ever the pragmatist, Chris observed that if I was committed to making more sophisticated beers, I first needed to learn a good deal more about the tools and ingredients of brewing. Sound advice.

From home brew stores, friends, the library, and mail order houses, I collected a dozen British and American professional and home brewing books. These volumes varied widely in their detail, emphasis, and, alas, their accuracy. If I got angry at myself for stupid or perverse mistakes, I was equally incensed by the confusing directions, oversimplification, and conflicting information some of these books provided. The worst was the one that promised to tell all one had to know about making beer in forty-two pages. Another book defined ale and lager without any reference to the different types of yeast employed. Some texts said one needn't boil the wort; others prescribed boiling at all costs. When I turned to professional brewing texts to mediate these squabbles, they were often too complicated to understand. The sad conclusion I reached was that there's much truth to the cliché about experience being the best teacher.

But, as with religion, you can't just walk into the first or second church you see and expect to find salvation. You have to search around. I did read a number of books that were both accurate and informative.

Several books recommended taking careful notes. When I looked back at my notes on the first twenty-odd batches, I was appalled at their skimpiness. As a professional journalist who supposedly knows how to take notes, I found these scribblings little more than lists of ingredients. At best, I'd thrown in snippets like "a curious, almost sour smell," or a plaintive "don't know if this was the right process." Also lacking was any evaluation of the results, or comparison of batches from the same recipe. Indeed, there was no comment at all on the beer's taste. In sum, these notes were barren of information I could draw upon for improvement. With such scanty records, I was not much better off than the prehistoric shaman who saw brewing as magic beyond his control.

In between the brewing texts, I read some more brewing history. In Michael Jackson's *The World Guide to Beer,* I learned that the most important date in the evolution of the beverage was the year 1516. One year before Martin Luther nailed his ninety-five theses on the castle door at Wittenberg and launched the Protestant Reformation, there occurred in Bavaria an event of similar gravity. Needing money for a military campaign, the Elector of that duchy decided to use the brewing industry as a source of revenue. In order to do that, he distinguished Bavarian beer from its host of competitors by governing its quality. The Purity Order, or *Reinheitsgebot,* stipulated that Bavarian beer could contain only malted barley, hops, and water (the yeast was assumed, though not named). This law has been adhered to in most of

Germany for five centuries and has done as much as anything to preserve a worldwide standard of beer quality and excellence. While beers of other nations have been altered, sweetened, colored to improve their appearance, or doused with chemicals to make them travel well or survive months on a shelf, the Bavarians have continued to brew on the straight and narrow.

Twenty-six years after the *Reinheitsgebot,* in a book called *A Compendious Regyment or a Dyetary of Health* (1542), the Englishman Andrew Boorde wrote: "Ale is made of malte and water; and they the which do put any other thynge to ale than is rehearsed, except yest, barme, or godesgood, doth sofysticate theyr ale." Unfortunately, Boorde was only a commoner and his injunction never attained the force of law.

So, to the ingredients.

Barley

Barley is a grain of multiple uses in cereal, soups, and cattle feed, but its primary value is in brewing. Raw barley cannot be transformed directly into alcohol. The starches in the grains must first be converted into sugars on which the yeast works to produce alcohol and carbon dioxide.

Barley is either two-row or six-row, depending upon the configuration of the kernels. The former has a higher starch content, paler color, and fewer enzymes. The latter has less starch but more protein. About 80 percent of the barley grown in the United States is six-row. Its use has historically meant that American brewers were able to harness excess enzymes to convert starches in other grains, such as rice and corn, and thus produce a lighter, clearer, and more stable beer.

The first step in this conversion process is malting, which the professional brewing manual *The Practical Brewer* defines as: "the controlled germination of barley during which enzymes are formed and food reserves (starches) are sufficiently modified so they can be further hydrolyzed (dissolved) at mashing."

The malting process is too complicated for all but a tiny group of home brewers. In fact, in this country, only Coors and some of the older Budweiser breweries do their own malting. All the rest are customers of huge malting companies.

The malting of barley takes place in three stages: steeping the raw grain, partial germination, and drying. The process lasts from five to twelve days, depending upon the kind of barley and the variety of malt sought. During germination, the starch portion of the grain is softened and made porous, and enzymes are distributed throughout. English two-row malts are germinated at lower temperatures and for longer periods of time than lager malts because fewer enzymes are available.

The beer's final aroma and color are determined during the kilning, or drying, phase. The higher the temperature, the darker the color of the final product. Black malt, used in stouts, is literally roasted, giving it a smoky, burnt taste.

Think of the maltster as a cross between a drill instructor and a quartermaster. Through a careful mixture of time, temperature, and moisture, he trains and supplies his enzyme and starch troops.

Theoretically, there is a great range of malts, but most brewers, even in Europe, stick to two or three. Malt available to American home brewers is likely to be six-row, prepared for the lager market. This means the all-grain brewer will probably need to add an extra step to his mashing and adapt his English texts accordingly. It is important for the American home brewer to know what kind of malt he's bought because most of the brewing texts are based upon the English system, utilizing English two-row barley.

The American home brewer is usually limited to the types of malt listed below:

Pale malt. The most common and widely used malt, dried at a temperature of around 175° F., which stops germination without killing the enzymes.

Amber malt. Dried at 230°, which kills both the embryo and some enzymes and imparts a slightly burnt taste to the beer.

Caramel or crystal malt. Partially dried, rewetted with a sugary water, then heated to 250°. Some fermentable sugars are developed during this process, but more importantly, the heat carmelizes the outer coating and gives the grain a rich, nutty flavor.

Black or chocolate malt. Roasted at 450°, which kills all the enzymes and adds a burnt flavor most commonly found in stouts.

    Both commercial brewers and all-grain home brewers develop their own flavors by blending some of the amber, crystal, or black malts with the basic pale variety.

Adjuncts

If you use dextrose for more than priming, you are adding an "adjunct" to the malt. This is the generic term for any grain or grain sugar besides malt that is added to beer. Elementary home brew recipes which prescribe one can of malt and four cups of dextrose contain about the same malt-to-adjunct ratio as most American beers. I don't use dextrose at all anymore except for priming because I prefer the all-malt taste and body. In the words of *The Practical Brewer*, "Adjunct use results in beers of lighter color, with a less satiating, snappier taste, greater brilliance, enhanced physical stability and superior chill-proof qualities. These attributes became extremely important with the advent of packaged beer."

    I used to believe the conspiracy theory that American beer had become progressively weaker and contained more (and cheaper) adjuncts simply because the brewing companies found they could make more money that way, and the public was too dumb to know the difference. I still think this is a factor. But I don't believe that the customer has been completely hoodwinked. He (and increasingly she) does want a less filling beer. The only way to provide it is to cut down on the calories, alcohol, and body.

    Most American beers contain between 30 and 40 percent adjuncts. Some of these substitutes are corn grits, flaked barley, oats, and wheat. But the big two are corn and rice. I have done no experimentation with adjuncts except to try flaked barley several times in valiant, ill-starred attempts to match Guinness's creaminess. Some of the English texts, especially Dave Line's *Big Book of Brewing*, treat adjuncts extensively. As far as I can see, the only reason for using them is to come closer to American beer—and that is just what I am trying to avoid.

There are, however, some additions to the basic four ingredients of beer that I find perfectably acceptable:

Yeast nutrients. Proteinous compounds useful when wort contains less than 60 percent malt.

Irish Moss. A seaweed, added during the last minutes of the boil. It helps coagulate haze-forming substances so they settle out.

Gelatin. The natural basis of Jell-O, which is added to aging beer to help clear it. Grocery store gelatin is as effective as the specially packaged "finings" in home brew stores.

Vitamin C. Useful as an anti-oxidant in aging beer.

Salt. Provokes bitter debate among home brewers. Most say a half or one teaspoon of noniodized salt per five-gallon batch is beneficial as a taste enhancer. Others, notably David Miller, inveigh against it as sin incarnate. I use a pinch and my beer seems to benefit slightly.

Water

Beer is mostly water. The extract brewer doesn't have to worry too much about the kind of water he uses, as long as it tastes and smells okay.

With all-grain brewing, water is much more important, and the first rule about it offends common sense: don't use the distilled variety. One would think that pure water would be the solution to questionable wells or inconsistent public water supplies. Unfortunately, this is a case where purity is not rewarded. I found this out when I brewed a couple of batches in Grand Rapids with distilled water and got very dull beer for my pains. You need the minerals for good beer.

Mashing, boiling, and fermentation are chemical reactions that depend upon certain chemical constituents of the water in which they occur. The mashing reaction should take place under slightly acidic conditions, between 5.2 and 5.7 pH, because those are the optimum conditions for the release and work of the enzymes. Since most municipal water is close to neutrality, or 7.0, the brewer needs to lower the pH (raise the acidity). The principal chemical reaction occurs when gypsum or calcium sulphate reacts with the phosphorus in the malt to produce calcium phosphate, which settles out, and phosphorous acid, which encourages the mashing reactions.

Those different enzymes that the maltster trained and preserved work best under special conditions. They are like troops that can fight well in the snows or the tropics, but not well in both. Dave Line has an image that helps clarify the division of labor between the two enzymes working on the barley. Picture two woodcutters. The first is a starch cutter, or Alpha enzyme, who works best cutting up the big starch logs at a certain temperature. His companion, the Beta enzyme, cuts best on the smaller sticks at lower temperatures. To complete both parts of the conversion of starches into sugars, therefore, requires both enzymes to operate at a compromise temperature which happens to be roughly 150° F.

Don't lose sight of your goal: to make good beer. That reminder holds especially true for explorations into the arcana of water treatment. You are not running a chemical laboratory. If I go to a lot of trouble to change the chemicals in my water with no improvement in the taste of my beer, what have I accomplished? People who drink it do not care about the sulphate ions or the pH level; they care about the appearance and taste of the beer.

After years of experimenting with different water treatments, I have concluded that the KISS principle (Keep it Simple, Stupid) works best. Assuming I am using municipal water (Burlington's has improved at last) that is soft and neutral, I add two teaspoons of gypsum to five gallons of water for pale ales or lagers, one and a half teaspoons for porters or steam beers, and none for stouts. The amount of gypsum differs because the darker malts already possess adequate acidity and therefore may be brewed in soft water. Pale beers, on the other hand, require hardened water to promote complete mashing.

It is good to remember the words of Professor Michael Lewis, who teaches fermentation sciences at the University of California at Davis. "Many people get hung up on water treatment when they should be working on their sanitation problems. The latter is something they really can affect."

Hops

Until I started brewing, my sole mental association with hops came from George Orwell's essay on hop-picking in Kent during the Depression. It is a grim account of long hours, exploitation, pitiable wages, and physical discomfort. There is not one word about drinking or making beer. "One's hands get stained as black as a negro's with the hop juice, which only mud will remove, and after a day or two they crack and are cut to bits by the (spiny) stems of the vines." Orwell earned about 10 shillings, or $2.00, a week.

Hops turn simple, sweet beer into complex and bitter ambrosia. The first use of hops came from brewers' restless search for different flavors and, more importantly, for substances that would sterilize and preserve their fragile beverage. Before the sixteenth century, hops were recognized for their soporific qualities and were stuffed in pillows.

Hops are members of the same biological family as *Cannabis sativa* (marijuana), but lack the latter's mind-altering powers. Long found wild in most temperate climates, hops are a perennial, bisexual vine with a phenomenal growing capacity, sometimes six inches a day. When cultivated, they are trained along wires or trellises and may grow thirty feet in a season.

For the brewer, the important part of the plant is the female flower. These green cones (or strobiles) are roughly the size of an acorn and look like pineapples. They serve three functions in brewing:

1. In their yellow lupulin powder lie the alpha and beta resins, which provide bitterness and a sterilizing quality to the beer. They are released during the vigorous boiling cycle. They contain no odor and settle out during the subsequent fermentation.

2. The essential oils impart a distinctive aroma for each variety of hops. This flavor is destroyed during the boil. Therefore, some hops are always added to the wort at the end of the boil, so the aroma may be gently released and trail off during fermentation and aging. The brewer keeps his best hops for this duty, to take full advantage of the delicate, fresh flavor. This is why hops are divided into two general

classes: boiling or bittering hops; and flavoring, aromatic, or finishing hops. As Fred Eckhardt recommends, hops should be added in inverse ratio to their freshness. "Buy hops when they are freshly harvested and store (freeze) them yourself. Don't trust shopkeepers!" he enjoins.

3. Hops also contain tannins that coagulate with the haze-forming proteins and carry them to the bottom during the boil and fermentation.

Hops are marketed in three forms: loose, pellets, and extracts. Loose hops are stripped from the vine and packed into two-hundred-pound bales, or "pockets." In pellet form, they look like rabbit food and are stronger than the loose.

Given the lack of clout home brewing shop retailers have with the hops merchants, it is probably better for the home brewer to choose pellets over loose. They are usually packaged in a vacuum and are therefore fresher than loose hops. There are few things more depressing to the serious home brewer than entering a store and seeing plastic bags of loose hops sitting in the direct light. If they were fresh and green when they arrived, they would soon be transformed into dry, brownish leaves as ugly in their own way as peroxided hair. Home brew stores are already at the end of the hops supply line. This retail negligence compounds the felony. Of course, if you live in Oregon or Washington state, where most hops are grown, or have some friendly brewer nearby who will sell them to you fresh, then use them. But most of us are not that fortunate.

Extracts offer a concentrate of hops bitterness without the aroma of any particular variety. I don't see any advantage in extracts. Even the poorest loose or pelletized hops will have some flavor, and bitterness alone doesn't make for good beer.

Commercial brewers buy hops according to an objective measure known as bitterness units. However, very few home brew retailers use this standard, which means that you have no way of knowing whether you are getting the same strength each time you buy hops, even within the same variety. This might change if enough home brewers and retailers complained to their suppliers, but in the meantime I suggest you stick to a few varieties from the same suppliers and experiment until you know their characteristics.

Some of the elementary home brewing texts make recommendations that, in the interests of simplicity, are very misleading. Many recipes call indiscriminately for "two ounces" of three or four kinds of hops, on the assumption that at least one will be available in the store the reader patronizes. That's fine. What they don't say, however, is that a particular variety may have twice the bitterness by weight as another. (It is like assuming that Kents and Camels have the same amount of nicotine.) The second glaring omission is the failure to indicate that hops pellets by weight are one-third stronger than the same variety in loose form. Using a full two ounces makes for overhopped beers.

If the home brewer wishes to buy loose hops, he should look for the following characteristics: the color should be green or greenish yellow, with lemon-colored lupulin powder evident; the aroma should be clean, without any earthy or sulphury smell; and the texture should be springy, not crackly or mushy, and have a smooth "rub." Your friends may be impressed to hear you are using Saaz or Styrian loose, but if the hops are three years old and have spent two of them in the hold of the *Flying Dutchman*, you are fooling no one but yourself. Better to buy fresh domestic Cascades or Clusters.

In spite of these caveats, I would say that there is more fun and challenge in experimenting with different hops than any other part of brewing. To the commercial brewer, consistency is the greatest virtue, but the home brewer can revel in the variety he gets with every batch. I know I do.

Some of the better known hops varieties are listed below:

Cluster. The quintessential North American hop, used in almost all American beers. Over 85 percent of the American hops production is Cluster. It has medium bitterness (7.5 percent alpha acid) and a stark aftertaste that can be off-putting.

Cascade. Lower bitterness (5.0 percent alpha acid) with a fine, flowery aroma. It can be used both for flavoring and finishing. I prefer it in loose form for the latter function.

Hallertau. The German lager hop from Bavaria and a firm friend. This is my favorite because it is the first one I used after I weaned myself off hopped malt extract. It serves equally well as a bittering and a finishing hop. It is mild but distinctly spicy, with a bitterness of 6.8 percent. I also use it in stout.

Tettnanger. A cousin of the Hallertau, grown in the Lake Constance region of Germany and not widely available in the United States. It has a low acid content and light bouquet.

Fuggles. The workhorse of English beers. Despite its weak resistance to infection and its low acid content, it is very popular with home brewers in both England and the United States. It has a definitely murky smell. Fred Eckhardt tells me fresh Oregon Fuggles are wonderful.

Talisman. Higher acid content and more pungent than Cluster (8 percent alpha acid). It is a good bittering hop.

Bullion. The Rocky Marciano of hops. Not much subtlety, strong, and very bitter (9 percent alpha acid and higher), it should never be used alone. It is excellent for stouts and porters. Brewer's Gold is a very similar hop.

Northern Brewer. Also possesses a robust acid content (8 percent and higher). Fritz Maytag uses it for Anchor Steam Beer. A wonderful hop when combined with Cascade or Hallertau for finishing.

Goldings. A favorite for English mild and bitter ales, but not widely available in the United States. It has a low acid content.

Saaz. The hop for the most famous lager in the world, Pilsner Urquell, and synonymous with Bohemian beers. When fresh, it has a stunningly spicy and pungent taste that perfectly complements the all-malt pale pilsners of Czechoslovakia. Hard to find in the United States.

The past hundred years has seen a steady decline in the amount of hops in American beer. In 1880, U.S. brewers added about four-fifths of an ounce of hops per gallon. By 1946 that amount had decreased by two-thirds. Today, it is about one-fifth of an ounce per gallon. This drop in the hopping rate has exactly paralleled the increased use of adjuncts, because the main function of hops is to balance the malt flavor. As the ratio of malt to other sweeteners has fallen, so has the amount of hops. Anchor Steam Beer, the only major all-malt commercial beer in America, still contains about four-fifths of an ounce of hops per gallon.

Yeast

"Beware the leaven of the Pharisees, which is hypocrisy." (Luke 12:1)

The writers of the Old and New Testaments called yeast leaven. The Greeks dubbed it *zestos*, meaning "boiling." Early English brewers called it Godisgood.

Yeast, we now know, is one of the simplest forms of plant life. This single-celled fungus, through very complex chemical reactions, converts sugars into carbon dioxide and alcohol. A single cell may reproduce thirty times before it dies. Over five hundred types of yeast have been isolated, not including the many wild strains that are always present in the air, but the brewer only uses two: the top-fermenting *Saccharomyces cerevisiae* and the bottom-fermenting *Saccharomyces uvarum*.

Top-fermenting yeast works on the surface of the beer at temperatures between 55° and 80° F. It has a higher alcohol tolerance—i.e., it can produce beer with higher alcohol content. It does not convert the dextrins well, so the resulting beers are sweeter. It is used in English ales, porters, and stouts.

Bottom-fermenting yeast is more fragile, works at lower temperatures (down to 33° F.), and has less alcohol tolerance, but it settles more readily, converts dextrins more completely, and makes for a brighter beer. This is the yeast for lagers.

Beer writer Michael Jackson suggests that it was the "advent of mechanical refrigeration which permitted brewers to hold lower temperatures needed for good bottom-fermentation, which, in turn, helped to promote lager, rather than ale, as the more universally popular beverage."

Alcoholic fermentation can take place with or without oxygen. In the presence of oxygen, yeast will rapidly convert sugar into carbon dioxide and alcohol. In oxygenless conditions, conversion is much slower. The brewer must first get the yeast working quickly (with oxygen), then cut off the air supply and let the yeast reproduce throughout the remaining wort without exposure to air. Fermentation then will continue until all the sugars are converted, or the alcoholic content has reached a level to inhibit further conversion. The home brewer can easily see the two stages of yeast production. In the primary fermenter, he looks for the high, craggy, protective head of foam and carbon dioxide. The ale ferment will make for a very craggy head (in lager, it will be a bit lower and smoother). Then he "shuts the door" of his cask or secondary fermenter to external oxygen and, not incidentally, to airborne bacteria and wild yeasts which would spoil the flavor.

Before Louis Pasteur, Emil Hansen, and yeast labs, there were the lees—accumulated yeast, proteins, and hops cells left as a scum in the fermentation vessel when the beer was transferred to aging casks. The English developed a practice of skimming their yeast off the top of the ferment and saving it for the next batch. Almost all English commercial brewers sell a concentrate of this extra yeast froth to make Marmite, a beef-essence paste that is spread on toast.

Breweries live or die by their yeasts. They spend great time and effort culturing and maintaining particular strains. They look at a variety of factors, such as the yeast's growth characteristics, fermenting power, and its ability to latch onto other cells which will carry it to the bottom as a sediment. As the two principal styles of brewing developed, the English learned to skim the middle portion of the foamy head atop their ales and porters, while the Continental and American brewers waited until the end of the lagering ferment to retrieve the yeast that had fallen to the bottom. Some brewing texts advise the home brewer to do the same thing.

Based on my experience—and the section on yeast contamination in *The Practical Brewer*—I do not recommend saving yeast, particularly when making lager. One cell of wild yeast in 16 million cells will make the beer hazy. Other contaminants are lactic acid and acid bacteria.

"It is not possible," *The Practical Brewer* contends, "to set fixed limits for the degree of infection which may be tolerated, as the conditions are different in every brewery. It is obvious that the biological purity of yeast goes hand in hand with the cleanliness of the plant and sterility of the equipment. For that reason it is necessary to employ the strictest cleaning and sanitation procedures in order to establish and maintain practical sterility. This point cannot be stressed enough."

I doubt that any but a handful of home brewers are willing or able to establish the sterile conditions necessary for carrying yeast from batch to batch. Whatever the drawbacks of commercial yeast packets (and some do get contaminated), the conditions under which they are produced cannot be matched by the home brewer. I, for one, will continue to use the powdered commercial yeasts together with a good "starter" program.

Fermentation goes much more easily when the yeast gets a running start. I use a system that is halfway between sprinkling the powdered yeast directly on the surface of the liquid and a much more elaborate arrangement recommended by Fred Eckhardt.

After about ten to fifteen minutes of the boil, I draw off about a cup of wort, cool it, and add my two packets of yeast. I pour this into a sterile half-gallon jug, give it a good shake, and attach a fermentation lock. By the time I have cooled the entire wort, the yeast starter is working well and ready to be pitched. Eckhardt says one should start the yeast two to three days before brewing, but I have not found that it makes any difference.

Yeast for home brewers comes in several forms:

Agar slant. Cultured yeast in a tube. This is hard to get and very expensive.

Pressed yeast. The form in which breweries culture and preserve their own yeast or the yeast they buy from laboratories. It's hard for the amateur to obtain.

Liquid yeast. Cultured in solution and shipped from the supplier in this form. I have never had much success with it, and it always needs a starter.

Dry, granulated yeast. The form most home brewers are familiar with. The packet will indicate whether it's top-fermenting or bottom-fermenting.

Yeast tablets. Supplied by some English brewing companies, but not widely available in this country.

Baker's yeast. Differs from brewer's yeast in that it was developed to produce the maximum amount of carbon dioxide to make the dough rise. In addition, baker's yeast doesn't ferment well at temperatures lower than 80° F., and the higher the temperature, the more vulnerable the wort becomes to infection. Baker's yeast hangs in the wort and makes for cloudy beer. Finally, bread yeast acts faster and produces a harsh, cidery, "yeast bite."

What I call Prohibition Pilsner beer, made with Blue Ribbon malt, cane sugar, and baker's yeast, is famous for its yeasty taste. Fred Eckhardt estimates that half the home-brewed beer made in this country is still fermented with baker's yeast because so many people see no reason to change; they are not experimenters, they are drinkers. Baker's yeast does work, and it is available in just about every general store from Yakima to Caribou. However, I find it hard to imagine being satisfied with the kind of beer it produces.

If I lived near a commercial laboratory that sold yeast slants or liquid yeast, I might be less skeptical of these. If I had a friendly brewer who would slip me an occasional twenty to thirty pounds of Karastan amber malt, I would use that. If I lived in the Yakima valley of Washington, my approach to hops would be different. However, none of these possibilities exists for me or for most home brewers.

It is important to remember that good ingredients will not rescue your beer from bad technique, but proper methods and the right equipment may make up for inferior (though not infected) ingredients. It is to equipment that we now turn.

Equipment:
From Bleach to Brew

To produce consistently good beer, you need the proper tools, equipment, and technique.

Home brewing equipment may be divided into three classes: that required for good extract brewing; that needed for all-grain brewing; and extras that may be useful or just plain fun to have.

The malt-extract brewer wants simplicity, low cost, replicability, and reliability. He likes making beer the way he likes a weekly game of golf. He wants to do it time and again, and he doesn't want to have to stop and fiddle with his gear each week.

The all-grain brewer, too, may reach the stage of producing beer as a habit. But he has a questioning turn of mind that keeps him looking for improvements. It may take him four or five hours longer for each brew, but he knows his product will be significantly better than anything he can buy and he is willing to invest in equipment that won't let him down. The all-grain brewer is like the bear who goes over the mountain—there is always one more thing to see, to buy, or to experiment with.

The third level includes fantasy or luxury equipment: lust for a copper boiler; craving for a bigger stainless-steel pot; desire for things that will improve the aesthetics of brewing, but bear little relation to the actual product.

Over 90 percent of America's home brewers use malt extracts exclusively, either syrup or powder. These brewers may experiment with different ingredients and recipes, but they are all variations on the same procedure.

Equipment for Extract Brewing

Here is all the equipment necessary to make respectable extract beers, based on standard batches of five gallons.

Boiler. Despite what a couple of texts say, you cannot make decent beer without boiling the primary ingredients. Therefore, you need a vessel of two or three-gallon capacity for carrying out the marriage of sweet wort and bitter hops. This may be a steamer, spaghetti cooker, or soup pot. Stainless steel is the best, and most expensive. I have also used enamel canning pots and aluminum cook pots, but I don't like the feel of the latter and the former often chip. I agree with Byron Burch: you have to find your own balance of quality, cost, and convenience.

Primary fermenter. This must allow for at least seven gallons to provide room for the initial vigorous bloom of fermentation. For years, home brewers used earthenware or stone crocks, but these are heavy when filled, hard to clean (even when new), and chip easily. The infections that such vessels often contain are carried over from batch to batch and help to give home brew a bad taste and a bad name. Avoid them.

Some books suggest using a clean plastic garbage can. From personal experience, I know this is bad advice. You don't know what kinds of chemicals go into cheap plastic. Remember, too, that alcohol is a solvent and its action on certain plastics can ruin beer. Beer is a food and deserves a home in a food-grade container. Further, get one with a lid. It need not be airtight. I know it's exciting to peer through cheesecloth or clear plastic to watch the fermentation, but beer making is better without kibbitzing. I put fifty batches of lager, ale, and stout through the bucket I bought from Tallmadge Nichols in Grand Rapids and it is still serviceable, although discolored by the hops resins. Be careful not to scratch the interior and thus build a home for bacteria.

Secondary fermenter. To house the quieter, slower, second stage of fermentation, the ideal container is the five- or six-gallon glass carboy. Any decent home brew store will sell it. You may also find one in antique stores or flea markets. The cost will range from $10 to $20. Carboys are easy to rinse out with chlorine solution or sodium metabisulphite. No harm can come to beer in a carboy, so long as it is corked with a bubbler/fermentation lock containing water.

In ten years, I have only broken one carboy—when I tried to use it as a primary fermenter. I assumed that the glass was equivalent to Pyrex and could withstand boiling liquids. As I poured some of the 210° F. wort into it, I heard a slight crack. I looked up and down the glass to inspect for breaks, but nothing was visible, so I poured in the rest of the wort. When it was time to move the carboy closer to the faucet to add some cool water, I lifted it up and about three gallons of wort flowed out over the floor. The glass had cracked all the way around the base, leaving nothing more than a shallow dish. Enough of the sides remained to hold about two quarts of liquid that did not join the rest spreading its amber stickiness across the floor. Moral: add some cool water to the wort first because a carboy cannot stand much more than 150° F.

Incidentally, pay heed to your back when you lift a carboy. It weighs a good fifty pounds when full, and two cases of the best beer will not compensate for a wrenched back or a hernia.

Blow-by. The reason I have stopped using a plastic bucket for a primary fermenter is that I have learned from Professor Michael Lewis and Al Andrews how to make beer entirely in glass carboys. The blow-by technique has several advantages and no drawbacks that I can discern. A blow-by is nothing more than a piece of plastic tubing of one-inch interior diameter (available by the foot at any good hardware store) that is wedged into the top of the carboy, curves down over the edge, and ends in a bucket of water or sodium metabisulphite solution.

The blow-by allows the first, turbulent fermentation to blow out carbon dioxide and a froth of yeasty foam and hops without permitting air to get back into the wort and contaminate the beer. This process will continue for one to three days. When it is time to transfer the wort to the secondary fermenter, I simply siphon it into another clean carboy, or I may leave it in the original one. I have found that beer made this way tastes noticeably smoother than previous batches made with the same ingredients. The greatest advantage of the blow-by is the improvement in sanitation. Once the plastic tube is in place, there is no way for bacteria to get into your beer. By leaving the beer in a single carboy for the entire ferment, you avoid possible contamination which might otherwise occur in transferring it to a secondary fermenter. It's just one less time that the beer is at risk.

The initial fermentation will blow out between two and five quarts, depending upon whether you use top- or bottom-fermenting yeast, the temperature of the brew at the time of pitching, and how full the carboy is. This is one of those matters for trial and error. I would suggest that you fill the carboy only up to the point where it narrows and see how much is blown out. The ideal is to blow off only the hops and proteins.

If you add water to make up the difference and want the final strength to equal that of the traditional two-step method, you'll need to add about 10 percent more hops and malt to the original recipe.

Fermentation lock. Also called airlock or bubbler. Hats off to the inventor of this simple device which allows fermentation to proceed undisturbed by the intrusion of nefarious wild yeasts or other airborne spoilers. When filled with water, it permits carbon dioxide to bubble off while excluding outside air.

In the days before fermentation locks, choosing the time to bottle was an art akin to a farmer's decision on when to plant. Littleton Long and Leonides Jones, both professors of English at the University of Vermont, have been brewing with the same recipe for some thirty years. According to their instructions: "Since there are so many variables, the safest indication of bottling time is the appearance of the brew itself. After the period of scum or foam formation is past, bubbles the size of a pin head will be seen bursting through the surface and going half an inch in the air. Gradually these will diminish in frequency and in size (to pin point dimension) and irregular islands or patches of thin foam will appear on the surface. The bubbling at this stage might best be described as a mist slowly rising to the surface. This is technically called 'allowing the beer to go flat.' Catching the beer at this point calls for judgment based on several experiences. There is no danger in letting the beer get too flat; the danger lies in bottling too soon, for bottles will explode if the internal pressure becomes too great."

I use the bubbler instead of a hydrometer to tell me when to bottle because each time I open the fermenter I risk contamination. When the bubbles come less frequently than one every ninety seconds, I know it's time to bottle. Depending upon the ambient temperature and yeast used, this might take as little as six days or as long as five weeks. Be patient.

Dark plastic bags. Beer is light-sensitive, which is why traditional beer bottles are of amber or dark green glass. Once the beer is in the carboy, I slip a garbage bag over it and cut a small hole for the fermentation lock. Then I just lift the skirt to see how it's coming along.

There have been times when I have had seven carboys in constant use during the winter brewing season. Lined up against a basement wall, shrouded in black, they remind me of the Empire's squat troops in *Star Wars*. I do most of my brewing in the winter because the risk of contamination is less in colder temperatures and because summer is the time to be outside in the garden or working with my bees.

Siphon hose and spigot. Because of the yeasty sediment in both primary and secondary fermentation, you can't just pour the beer from one vessel to another through a funnel. Instead, you need four to six feet of clear plastic tubing with an inside diameter of about three-eighths of an inch to siphon it off with a minimum of agitation.

When I started brewing, the only method I could devise to control the flow of the liquid was to crimp the business end of the tubing with my fingers just as the beer reached the top of the receiving bottle. My timing was never very good and I used to spill three or four bottles' worth each time. There were (and are) plastic crimpers on the market, but they are very brittle and always break at inopportune moments. A metal tube with a spring-loaded opening was too slow. Finally, I found a good solution in a plastic stop cock that fits snugly onto the end of the tubing. You need two hands to use it, but it won't leak, break, or otherwise let you down.

Copper tubing. My system for transferring beer from fermenter to fermenter and on to bottles consists of a two-foot length of copper tubing (three-eighths of an inch in diameter) curved at one end like a cane. To the "handle" end I attach my plastic tube. The straight end of the copper goes down into the beer until it rides just above the level of the sediment. This is a variation of the stiff plastic tubes sold in some home brew stores.

Bottle brush. Almost every home brewing text recommends such a brush. I don't know why. If a bottle is so skuzzy or scummy that you need a brush to clean it, you should chuck it. A round brush is handy for cleaning the upper half of a carboy where bits of hops adhere and dry (it is too short to reach the bottom), but for bottles, no.

Bottles. They ring our kitchen, like the Parthenon's frieze—eighty empty beer bottles from thirty foreign countries and the United States. They are of all sizes and shapes. I drank most of them, and friends, knowing of my beery monomania, brought the rest from India, Nepal, and Belgium. Some I have used for my own beer in hopes that the interesting label on the outside would anoint the contents. I put my stout in Guinness bottles or my ale in Belhaven bottles in much the same spirit as I watch the Wimbledon finals to improve my tennis.

In my early brewing days, I didn't care about the size of bottles I used. I took what was available, a potpourri of squat Labatt's, tall Budweiser bar bottles, Piels pints, brown Tooth's Sheaf Stout from Australia (my favorites), distinctive porcelain-capped Grolsch flagons and Narragansett quarts.

As time went by, bottling lost its therapeutic appeal and I began looking for ways to simplify and speed up the process. Just as my source of the lovely Tooth's dried up (the distributor couldn't sell enough in northern Vermont), I discovered American champagne bottles— a free, steady supply of them. One day a radio ad promoting champagne breakfasts at a local motel penetrated my consciousness and spurred me to ask if I could have the empty bottles. I did feel rather grubby rummaging through garbage dumpsters to pull them out, but they were free. After a few weeks, the hostess took pity on me and saved them behind the bar. I found, however, that not all American brands took a crown cap, and none of the French varieties did.

In a trice, I cut bottling time by a third. Champagne bottles hold just over twenty-five ounces, so a five-gallon batch will require twenty-four instead of forty-eight bar bottles. It does mean that whenever I want a beer I must be very thirsty or share one with Chris, but that kind of problem is a pleasure.

Champagne bottles of home brew also make excellent gifts to beer-drinking friends. A single twelve-ounce bottle is not enough and a six-pack is perhaps more than you want to part with, while a champagne bottle is more than an afterthought but less than 5 percent of your whole batch. As long as the champagne flows on Sunday, I don't have to worry about retrieving the bottles, though good friends do save them for me and better friends return them washed.

I now use four sizes: twelve-ounce bar bottles, champagne bottles, my hoarded stock of Tooth's twenty-six-ouncers, and Grolsch flagons, which I get from a local bar that caters to singles.

Since Vermont has a deposit law, all bottles are returned to grocery stores or beverage centers. I have "bought" bottles from these centers at a nickel apiece, but getting them this way makes me queasy. Out of each case, you are likely to find at least one that's been used as an ash tray. The most loathsome aspect of home brewing is the washing out a stranger's cigarette butts.

A better solution is to buy commercial beer in bar bottles or heavy-duty pints or quarts. You will know that the bottles are clean because you drank the contents.

Don't use no-return bottles because the glass is not strong enough to hold well-primed home brew, and don't use those with twist-off caps. The brewery can get a tight seal, but you won't.

Capper. There are several on the market, including one bizarre style that requires a hammer. I still use the same bench capper I bought ten years ago in a tiny hardware store. It cost about $6 and was the most expensive item I had to buy for my brewing. Today, it runs over $25. Mine has capped over four thousand bottles without a miss. Keep your eye out at yard sales and flea markets. If you buy a bench capper, make sure it has a cotter pin on the arm for adjusting to the height of the bottle.

Always fill bottles to within an inch or an inch and a half from the top. Never cap half-full bottles. Contrary to common sense, they build up much greater pressure than those with a proper amount of head space.

One can't discuss bottles without considering cleanliness. The three cardinal rules of good brewing, according to Michael Lewis, are "sanitation, sanitation, and sanitation." I know of one Prohibition-style brewer who says the only way he ever cleans his bottles is to wash them out with hot water after every use. Then he stores them upside down. He claims he has never had infected beer, but I'm not sure I believe him. It is almost impossible to taste the difference between contaminated and cidery brew. He is right, however, to wash out his bottles as soon as they are empty to clean out the sediment on the bottom.

I have gone through quite a metamorphosis in my own cleaning technique. At one point I was washing bottles with water, rinsing with chlorine bleach, then rerinsing with sodium metabisulphite and again with water. The tedium of filling the bottles was a lark compared to the cleaning. Then I took Fred Eckhardt's advice. Fill a small bucket with water and add two tablespoons of household chlorine bleach per gallon. Soak everything in this—tubing, spoons, bottles, fermenters— and drip-dry. Whatever residue remains will be so diluted it won't affect the beer. Sodium or potassium metabisulphite, the customary sterilant, inhibits but does not kill bacteria. Don't rinse bottles or equipment after this sterilization. You may double or quadruple the bleach strength if you want, but then you should rinse lightly with a milder sterilant.

Thermometer. In making extracts, a thermometer's principal use is in finding the right temperature for adding the yeast and in knowing how much to adjust the hydrometer's reading as the wort temperature diverges from 60° F. Thermometers are much more important in mashing, for the brewer must take accurate readings between 120° and 180°. Candy or dairy thermometers fill this bill.

Hops bag. This is unnecessary if you use pellets, and questionable even with loose hops. By tying your hops in a bag, you lose some of their bitterness and flavor. Obviously, with loose hops, you do need some way to strain them out when you pour the wort into the primary fermenter.

Strainer. A stainless-steel colander, layers of cheesecloth, or a specially made filter bag available in some home brew shops makes a suitable strainer. Whether cloth or metal, the strainer should be clean.

Spoon. This may be either wood or stainless steel, at least twelve inches long. Stainless steel is easier to clean, but wood feels better.

Funnel. Required for pouring liquids such as yeast starters and sodium metabisulphite into the small opening of a carboy or bottle.

Pots and pans. Such as you would have around any kitchen to prepare priming sugar, gelatin, gypsum, etc.

Scale. The small postal variety is helpful for weighing hops.

Notebook. For the scientist, the injunction to take detailed, careful notes and not cheat on them is essential to experimentation. The sooner home brewers learn and practice this, the better. "Those who cannot remember the past are condemned to repeat it," wrote the philosopher George Santayana. Nothing is more certain than human readiness to forget a mistake and its causes. My own mind simply does not register lapses into sloth, cussedness, distraction, or errors of judgment. I must write down all my procedures. *Good records produce good beer.*

All-Grain Equipment

All-grain beer is only for those restless brewers eager to plunge into a welter of extra equipment, long hours, and more temperamental ingredients. It is not for the casual hobbyist.

A good sign that you are all-grain material is if you find yourself prowling around kitchen supply stores and junk yards. Every all-grain brewer I've met has some experimental and technical bent. This is vital, for you'll get little guidance from brewing texts and no firm agreement, even among brewers, on the best equipment for the job.

You must develop your own procedures and techniques. The all-grain brewer quietly stops talking about the economic attraction of brewing and concentrates on taste and technique.

Grinder. All-grain brewing begins with properly malted barley. Some home brewing shops will grind bulk grain for you and others sell small amounts at $2 a pound, which makes it 50 percent more expensive than extracts. Obviously that is not a good bargain.

I tried to buy bulk barley at a local feedstore, and they told me it was available only in railroad car lots and only in its unmalted state. I finally found that I could order 40- or 110-pound bags through the local food co-op.

Knowing how to grind the grain is at least as important as finding the machinery to do it. Food processors and coffee grinders produce too fine a powder. A blender makes it too coarse. The grain must be ground just enough to crack open the husks and expose the starch. During mashing, the starch is liquefied and removed from the husks. During sparging, the husks form a filter bed through which the sugary liquor drains, leaving the grain particles behind. Hal Boutelier built his own grinder by hooking up a hand mill to a ½-horsepower electric motor. That was beyond my skill. My two alternatives were to buy an electric grain grinder for $150 or a Corona hand grinder for about $30.

I had been told that grinding ten pounds of grain by hand would take an hour. To test this assertion, I took half a pound of grain to the store and timed myself: it took less than thirty seconds. Ten to eleven minutes for ten pounds seemed acceptable, so I bought the hand grinder and screwed it firmly onto the top of the workbench in the basement. In fact, I now rather enjoy those ten minutes spent grinding grain. I feel at one with the overworked and underappreciated camels of Mesopotamia and Egypt which have turned millstones for thousands of years.

Mashing vessel. A five-gallon batch of all-grain beer contains eight to ten pounds of grain. This must be mashed at a ratio of about a quart of water per pound. Since you will need to stir the mash a good deal, you want a vessel of three and a half- to five-gallon capacity. I found a used four-gallon stainless-steel soup kettle which should last me as long as I brew.

pH papers. These are useful if you want to measure and adjust the acidity of your mashing water. The scale between 4.8 and 7.0 is tricky to use if you, like me, are red-green color blind. But with some practice, you can get approximate readings. I must confess I hardly use them anymore because a slight variation in the acidity seems to make no difference between beers.

Sparging equipment. I spent more time experimenting with this stage of brewing than with all the others combined. It may have been my mechanical ineptitude; it may have been the inadequacy of the books I consulted. In any case, I offer my system, which now works adequately.

Sparging takes place after the malt enzymes have done their best to convert the starches to fermentable sugars. The aim is to rinse all the sugars out of the grain while leaving behind as much haze-forming protein material and husks as possible. My system requires two food-grade plastic buckets, such as those used in health food stores for tofu (but not for any kind of oil or peanut butter) or in doughnut shops for jelly. One should hold four gallons and the other six gallons. About an inch above the bottom of the larger bucket, I drill a hole and insert a plastic spigot such as you see on coffee urns. These spigots are available from restaurant supply stores and are easily installed. Next, I drill about two hundred $3/16$-inch holes in the bottom of the smaller bucket. This bucket slips snugly inside the larger one and rests about three inches off the bottom because the rim holds it at this level. The inner bucket serves as a false bottom by collecting the grains but allowing the sugar-laden water to pass through.

Sparge water vessel. For a five-gallon batch of beer, you need five to six gallons of sparging water at 170° F. Sparging takes thirty to forty-five minutes and you should not let the water drop below 160° during that time. I have a five-gallon canner, and as I use up some of the water, I add another gallon, keeping the temperature constant. Into this vessel I place my copper cane. To its curved end, I attach a plastic hose with a screw clamp. The hose extends down about eighteen inches to a plastic stop cock. Early in my sparging researches, I followed the advice of Dave Line, who recommended a spray head to disperse the sparging water evenly across the surface of the grain bed. When he further suggested that the sparging water should just cover the top of the grain bed, I said to myself, Why should I spray the water? So I didn't, and my results were just as good as before.

(Such minutiae may seem tedious to those readers who care little about actual brewing, but I hope it will encourage others to keep experimenting and testing all techniques in the boiler of their own experience.)

Using the plastic cock, I can adjust the intake of sparging water to match exactly the outflow through the spigot at the bottom of the larger mashing bucket. As soon as I begin sparging, I clean the mash pot and use that to collect the runoff.

When I have collected a total of three gallons of runoff I transfer it to the stove. By the time it is close to boiling, the sparging is usually complete and I can transfer the second three gallons to another pot on the stove. If I had a seven-gallon pot, I could do it all with one vessel.

Wort chiller. Like a football receiver fully extended to catch a pass, home brew is at its most vulnerable between the end of the boil and the time the yeast has built a protective layer of foam on the wort's surface. If you wait for hot wort to cool down by itself, it can take twelve to twenty hours. Even leaving the vessel outside in 20° weather in Vermont, it still takes eight hours to reduce it to yeast-pitching temperature. Immersing the vessel in cold water can do the trick in one to two hours, but manhandling fifty pounds of boiling-hot liquid is a risky proposition. Breweries cool their beer through heat exchangers. Could I do the same?

Not being a mechanical engineer, I had no answer until I met Al Andrews of Riverside, California. An engineer who tests equipment for the Navy, Andrews is an avid home brewer. He designed all his own equipment and sells some of it.

Before I bought his wort chiller, I would have listed it in an optional equipment category; after one use, it was moved to the necessary list. This device consists of twenty feet of copper tubing coiled

inside twenty feet of clear plastic hose with standard garden hose con-
nections at each end. The wort flows through the copper in one direction, and cold tap water flows through the plastic in the other direction. In about fifteen minutes, you can bring the $200 + °$ F. wort down
to 80° and pitch your yeast. It is a wonderful advance and worth every
penny of the $40 price.

Optional Equipment, Practical Fantasies

The search for better equipment is a trail of broken promises—the
same promises: "Once I have this valve [or this keg or this sparger],
I will be content." Alas, it doesn't work that way. The all-grain fever
of acquisition is a bit like malaria: once you contract it, you never
quite get rid of it. With self-restraint, however, you can keep it under
control.

The secret to good beer is to worry only about those factors that
will improve it. As Professor Lewis said in a 1982 lecture at Boulder,
"It is all very well to enthuse over Saaz hops or a fancy CO_2 system,
but unless you pay attention to sanitation, your beer will be bad. Sanitation is dull; but scrupulous, resolute, obsessive attention to cleanliness is far more important for good beer than all the fancy ingredients
and equipment you may assemble."

Bruheater. Unlike the wort chiller, which changed immediately from
fantasy to necessity, the Bruheater remained an optional piece of
equipment, even after three years of use. This English invention is a
six-gallon plastic vessel with its own heating element and rheostat for
controlling temperature. It may be used for mashing, boiling, and
heating sparging water. It costs $80, not counting the expense of con-
verting the English outlet to a three-prong 220-volt plug.

I have had mixed success with it in mashing because of the higher
protein levels of American malts. The Bruheater was designed for a
single infusion mash at 160° F. That is fine if you have well-modified
English malts. With American malts, mashing is incomplete without
a protein rest and a two-step infusion. You cannot step-raise temperatures in the Bruheater without burning some of the liquid and reduc-
ing the effectiveness of the heating coil. Consequently, I employ the

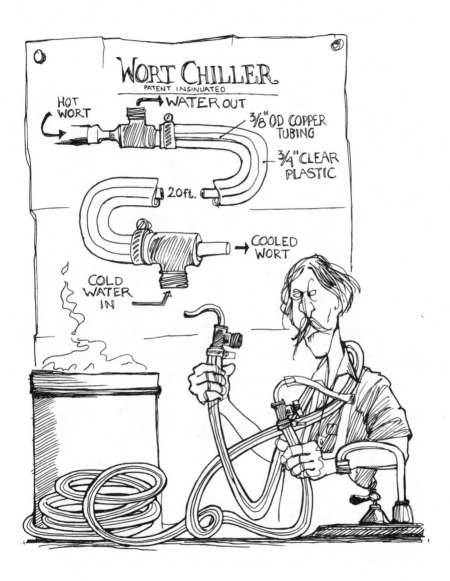

Bruheater for heating sparging water and boiling the wort, but not for mashing. It does have the advantage of requiring one less pot on the crowded kitchen stove and one less trip down a steep flight of stairs.

Bottle washer. This device, which fits over a water spigot and has a pressure-release action, sprays the inside of bottles with tap water. It costs about $15. If I have picked up bottles from an outside source, I first soak them in a chlorine bleach solution (one tablespoon per gallon) for half an hour. (Never use soap or detergents to clean bottles, as they wreak havoc on the beer's head.) Then I rinse them with the bottle washer before using sodium metabisulphite. A bottle washer is a time saver, but you can certainly do without it.

Kegs. No matter how much you love bringing out a bottle of home brew, there comes a time when you grow tired of cleaning and filling hundreds of bottles. Kegs can turn your basement into a pub, where your thirsty legs can carry you to tap a glass or pitcher with ease. At Burlington's only junk yard I found six used 7.75-gallon Narragansett quarter kegs at scrap metal prices—$10 apiece. I bought three. I didn't have the foggiest notion about how to clean them, where to get new bungs, or how to prime them. There was still some old beer sloshing around inside, and I decided it wouldn't hurt to clean them with caustic soda, which I begged from a local milk plant. I rinsed each keg well, poured in a sodium metabisulphite solution, and drained them.

Hearing my prayers, St. Gambrinus, the patron saint of brewing, decided to reward me for a good deed. One morning I called up the city streets department to compliment them for rapidly sanding an icy patch of road. I got into conversation with Bill Rockwell, the assistant superintendent, who then brought up the subject of home brewing because he had read about our attempts to mount a home brewing contest. One thing led to another and it turned out that he and a friend in the parks department had kegged three or four batches. They'd used the same size kegs I had and filled them with three-quarters of a ten-gallon batch. What's more, Rockwell had a CO_2 dispenser system that allowed him to drink beer from the keg for three or four weeks without its going flat.

Rockwell said his only disaster had occurred one night when he had a ten-gallon batch ready to transfer out of the primary into the keg. It was late and he decided to place his siphon hose with one end in the primary and the other in the keg and let it flow overnight. He woke up about two hours later after dreaming about beer, smelled beer, got out of bed, and went downstairs to find the kitchen floor awash. Somehow, one end of the siphon hose had flipped out of the keg and seven of the ten gallons had followed the laws of gravity first to the floor, then to the living room, and finally to the basement. It took most of the morning to clean it up, and the stink remained for months.

To fill my first keg, I simply mixed seven and a half gallons from a light and a dark ale I had aging in carboys. I found a bung at the hardware store, boiled it for five minutes, and pounded it home with a four-pound sledgehammer. Over the hot summer, the keg sat in our 60° F. basement until, at the end of August, we tapped it for the christening of our son. I rented a simple hand pump tapper system from a beverage store, and the beer was fine. Toward the end of the afternoon, as the natural CO_2 dissipated, the beer went a little flat, but its taste remained first-rate and we drank it to the lees.

Tapping and drinking an entire keg at one time is okay, but what about home draft beer? The only way to keep it carbonated is to buy a CO_2 pressure system. That can cost over $150—more than I had spent on all other equipment combined. Chris saved me the agony of justifying its purchase when she gave me one for Christmas. Now, I can't imagine brewing a keg without it. What pleasure, what ease to trip to the basement and return with a pitcher of cool foamy lager or ale!

Kegging does mean putting seven and a half gallons in one container; if it is not absolutely clean, you lose three cases of beer at one time.

Another challenge is how to chill a whole keg. Beer needs a steady temperature. Even ale requires a temperature between 50° and 55° F. Lifting a keg in and out of a deep freeze is hard on the back. Why not pick up a used refrigerator? That is getting closer to the pub idea, and if you are doing a lot of lagering you need a temperature below 40° anyway. Al Andrews keeps four 5-gallon Cornelius kegs in his refrigerator simultaneously, with a four-spigot tapper system. He can draw lager, ale, stout, or porter as the spirit and thirst moves him.

One day I drifted into an antique store specializing in restored clocks, instruments, tools, etc. In a corner there was a six-gallon copper boiler with top and brass spigot. My mind raced ahead to what a wonderful mash tun or lauter tun it would make. I looked at the price . . . and gagged: $280! Who needed a $280 pot?

The store owner saw my lustful expression begin to fade. "There's nothing special about a brass spigot," he said. "I'd love to sell it to you, but I'm a home brewer myself and I doubt if it would make your beer any better." My thoughts exactly, once I stopped caressing its shiny surface. Better to let some decorator buy it for a trendy restaurant and fill it with ferns.

Hal Boutelier built a cooler from plywood and Styrofoam and a used refrigerator motor. In it he keeps up to five carboys of lager at 35° F. for months. Jim Kollar, a home brewer in Virginia, refrigerated an entire room to keep cold his forty to fifty cases and kegs. He has since moved on to build the Chesapeake Bay Brewing Company, a micro-brewery in Virginia Beach. That is beyond my wilder fantasies.

You don't have to be an engineer to brew your own beer. But it helps to have an experimental bent, a quizzical streak, and a resolve to improve. I love the American Homebrewers Association dearly, and they have done more to promote the cause of good home brewing in this country than any other organization. But their motto bothers me: "Relax. Don't Worry. Have a Homebrew." When I am making beer, especially all-grain beer, I cannot afford to relax until the yeast has been pitched. Making beer is serious business. I would modify their motto to the less catchy, but (for me) more appropriate: "Pay attention. Worry intelligently. And have a homebrew when you're done."

The Practice
of All-Grain Brewing

My all-grain brewing begins with a hot cup of coffee. That's because it's 5:00 a.m. and I need to be wide awake when I enter the brewery-basement.

All of what follows involves a five-gallon batch, since most home brewers work with that amount. I always hope I will produce a beer that approximates the incomparable Pilsner Urquell. My grandparents emigrated to Montana from a town about a hundred miles east of Pilsen in Bohemia, and I shall call this beer Ma Vlast Lager (My Fatherland Lager) to honor my Czechoslovakian heritage. The recipe is my own variation on one in Dave Miller's excellent *Home Brewing for Americans*. He helped me make decent all-grain lager for the first time in my life.

I had ground ten pounds of six-row barley the night before. I buy the grain in 110-pound sacks about twice a year through my food co-op. It had taken six or eight tries to grind it just right with my Corona hand mill. The books told me to crack, not crush, the husks and expose the starchy innards while leaving the outer layer to make a filter bed during sparging.

I fire up my mashing water by heating ten quarts to 130° F. (one quart per pound of grain) in my four-gallon stainless-steel pot. I know from asking the city water department that my source of water has a neutral pH of 7.1 with medium hardness (120 parts per million of carbonates) and no sulphates. For this pale lager, I want a pH of 5.6, so I add three teaspoons of gypsum (calcium sulphate)—two teaspoons to the mash water and the other to the sparging water. The calcium sulphate reacts with the phosphorus in the malt to produce a weak phosphorous acid which lowers the pH. Such acidity is necessary for efficient mashing, good protein "breaks," and proper coagulation of proteins for a clear beer. I put the gypsum into a small saucepan of water, which I heat to boiling. Don't expect it to dissolve completely, because it won't.

Next I pour the ground grain into the mash water, stirring well with a long-handled spoon to break up any lumps. This is a dusty task regardless of how I cracked the grain. The temperature should fall to 120° to 122° F. and the mash will be the consistency of half-cooked oatmeal. I make sure the temperature is above 120°, put the lid on, and wait for fifteen to twenty minutes before checking again. This "protein rest" lasts forty-five minutes and is necessary to break down the protein so that later in the process it will settle out and not cause residual haze in the beer. I keep the temperature between 118° and 122° by judicious applications of heat and constant stirring. (Incidentally, this is far easier to do with gas than with electric burners.)

The first stage of mashing is the time to clean bottles if I am bottling another batch that day. I try to commingle brewing and bottling to make use of lag periods as I brew. To this end, I put three to four gallons of water and three tablespoons of chlorine bleach in my old primary fermenter and soak the bottles, plastic tubing, hydrometer, measuring cup, etc., to sterilize them. I let them drip-dry.

After forty-five minutes it is time to boost the mash temperature. Home brewing is not an exact science: at this point, two enzymes work in inexact tandem: the alpha enzymes chew into the malt starches best at about 147° to 155° F. and break them down into dextrins, which are largely unfermentable but add body to the beer. The beta enzymes convert dextrins to fermentable maltose or malt sugar at a temperature between 135° and 147°. A temperature of roughly 153° is the compromise for a single infusion mash for well-modified English malts. However, with less modified American malts, I must go through a two-stage process so that both alpha and beta enzymes have a chance to do their job.

In this recipe, I move up to the starch conversion temperature of about 155° F. within fifteen to twenty minutes, with a pause at 140° where the maximum sugar conversion takes place. To some extent, the brewer controls the final sweetness or dryness of the beer (the ratio of dextrins to maltose) by changing the length of time and the temperature during the mash. The main thing to remember is that if you push the temperature much over 155°, you risk killing the alpha enzymes. One reason commercial lagers have less body than ales is that they are mashed longer at lower temperatures where more fermentable maltose is produced.

During any application of heat, it is important that you stir constantly, or risk burning some of the grains on the bottom of the pot. It is also vital that you take constant and careful temperature readings, particularly as you approach 155° F. Take your readings in the middle of the mash, and if you have one of those thermometers with a metal ring around the bulb, avoid letting grains collect on it because they will give you a false reading.

After fifteen to twenty minutes at 155° F., I do the starch test. I put one or two drops of mash liquor on a clean saucer. Then I add a drop of medicinal iodine. If the color remains the iodine brown, starch conversion is complete. If the color turns blue, that means starch is still present and I leave the mash for another ten to fifteen minutes and then do a second test.

Assuming the test is positive, it is time to kill off the beta enzymes. If I don't do this, I will end up with too thin a beer, because all the body-building dextrins will convert to maltose and subsequently be fermented. The executioner in this case is more heat. I bring the temperature up to 168° F., stirring all the while. This stabilizes the ratio between maltose and dextrins in the beer.

At the risk of being pedantic, I remind you to write down what you do at each step so you can consider any changes you might want to make in the next batch.

In the middle of the second stage, I turn on the heat for my sparging water. I use my Bruheater with its six-gallon capacity and rheostat to heat the water to 175° F. If you don't have a Bruheater, you must juggle vessels on the stove to supply a total of five to six gallons of water at that temperature. Remember that sparging will take thirty to forty-five minutes and the water should remain above 170° for effective rinsing of the grains.

Now comes the part of brewing that used to give me ulcers— sparging. It reminds me of learning to drive. If you think of all the different motions and positions separately, it is almost impossible to imagine how they connect. Yet, once you learn to do it, the procedure is quite simple.

My mashing equivalent of a driver's education course was about ten batches of all-grain brewing over a six-month period. My sparging method works as follows: I put the Bruheater filled with six gallons of water on top of the clothes dryer (that's where the only 220-volt outlet in the house is located). Below it, on a sturdy stool, sit my mashing buckets, one inside the other. On the floor, under the spigot, is my stainless-steel mash tun for collecting the liquor runoff.

First I fill the space between the bottom of the outer bucket and the many-holed bottom of the inner bucket with about half a gallon of 175° F. water. This is to prevent a vacuum from forming as I draw off the first runnings. Then I ladle the grainy "goods" into the inner bucket, and give a couple of vigorous stirs. I pour in enough extra water to just cover the top of the grain. I let this stand five to ten minutes.

The reason for "underletting" the grains with water is explained by Michael Lewis: "You have a bunch of particles that are suspended in the wort you have produced. The particles are exhausted and the one thing you must not do is compact the bed. Don't begin the runoff right away. When you do, slide the wort out from among the particles and slide the sparge water in from the top. In other words, as you drain out the wort from the bottom, you add sparging water from the top. Gradually, you sneak up on the particles, replacing the wort in which they are suspended with hot water. If you simply draw out the wort too quickly, the bed will collapse and you will have a stuck mash."

A stuck mash is a brewer's nightmare. It is like letting wallpaper paste set too long. It means you have to dredge up all the "goods" and start the mash over again, a messy, time-consuming process that will affect the final maltose-to-dextrin ratio, not to mention your good humor.

I set up my tubing arrangement, from copper pickup in the Bruheater to plastic tube to stop cock. Next, I slowly draw off the first

cloudy runnings from the spigot in the lower mash bucket. When I
have a quart or so, I gently pour it back through the top of the grain
bed, draw off another quart, and repeat the process. I continue recy-
cling this liquor until it is the color of slightly soapy water. Then I
open the tap and let it drain directly into the collecting vessel on the
floor. I open my plastic stop cock so that the sparge water inflow (it
drizzles out rather than sprays) matches the outflow at the bottom. I
want to keep the water level just at the top of the grains. One can't
rush this process. I find that I can do other chores while the sparging
proceeds, so long as I watch the water level. It is an immense improvement over sparging with a ladle and colander.

When I have three gallons of liquor, I pour them into another pot
and place them on the stove to boil. I continue sparging until I have
another three gallons. (That is a total of six gallons for a five-gallon
batch because I expect to lose two to three quarts in steam and I want
to have a bit extra for starting the yeast.) I take the grains out to the
compost pile for next year's carrots and tomatoes.

The wort is heating up now, making the kitchen redolent with the
sweet smell of malt. Boiling kills off any residual alpha enzymes. When
the hops are added, the liquid will be well sterilized. The boil also
removes the haze-forming fraction of the beer, so that the end product
should be as refreshing to the eye as to the palate.

A watched pot *will* boil—more importantly, it *won't* boil over. To
clean up a boil-over is to swear off the sin of inattention forevermore.
Yet you need a good, rolling, kicking boil for fifteen to twenty minutes
before you're ready to add any hops. That time has come when the
malt proteins begin to coagulate into larger and larger clumps. This
"hot break" is one of the more dramatic (and at first sight unsettling)
phenomena in brewing. The proteins gather like storm clouds against
a gray-green sky. The first time I saw it happen, I thought something
was wrong and I dumped the batch.

Here I add one ounce of my Saaz pellets as bittering hops. Thirty
minutes later, I put in another half-ounce of the pellets. You must stand
there and control the burners to guard against a possible boil-over.
When the froth recedes, you can then adjust the heat to give a controlled, rolling boil. You will note that a second marriage is under way
as soon as the hops are added: the hops' tannins combine with the

malt proteins to form clumps which will eventually sink of their own weight.

Thirty minutes before the end of this ninety-minute boil, I add a teaspoon of Irish Moss, which further aids protein coagulation, and hence clearer beer.

After ninety minutes, I turn off the heat and put in my aromatic hops. I use either another half-ounce of Saaz pellets or three-quarters of an ounce of Hallertau loose. The brewer wants their flavor to rise above the bitterness of the boiling hops. These should be the freshest, most flavorful hops, for their smell will predominate in the beer.

Midway through the boil, I scoop out one to two pints of wort for my yeast starter. I force-cool this in the freezer, being sure to keep it covered. Once it reaches 75° F. (measured with a sterilized thermometer), I pitch in two packets of yeast (I use Vierka), cover the container, and place it in blood-temperature water. The yeast is working well by the time I have cooled the main wort.

After letting the wort rest for half an hour, I pour it through a fine mesh plastic cloth (sterilized), which catches the loose hops. Then I dip out a quart of the wort and pour it through one final time to snare the last sugars.

It is important to filter out the hops and as much of the proteinous materials as possible so that you don't clog the take-up tube in the next stage.

At this point I give the wort another vigorous stirring with a sterile spoon. This makes most of the suspended particles sink to the bottom and center of the vessel so they are not taken up in the copper tube.

Enter Al Andrews's wonderful wort chiller. I heft the five gallons of wort onto the clothes washer in the basement. Then I place my copper cane in the wort and connect it to the chiller by a piece of sterile plastic tubing. The chiller, which is fifteen inches across, sits in the basement sink. That allows me to connect the cold water faucet to the outer plastic cover with a short piece of garden hose. The open end simply drains into the sink. To the exit end of the copper tubing I attach another length of sterile plastic tube, which trails over the edge of the sink and into my carboy.

It is here that I dispense with the plastic bucket primary fermenter and use a blow-by (see Chapter 7). These two technical devices, the wort chiller and the blow-by, together with improved sanitation, have produced a seven-league advance in my brewing success.

I suck the wort through the chiller to get it started. I know that sucking may introduce germs, but I haven't been able to figure out a sterile alternative. Then I turn on the cold water tap and adjust it to give me an exit temperature for the wort of 80° F. or less. In fifteen minutes, all the wort has passed through the copper coil. I pour my started yeast into the carboy about halfway through the filling process. This is to get it well roused and working throughout the wort. In fact, it is important to make sure that all the wort flowing into the carboy is well roused with oxygen so the yeast will have a good sendoff into creativity and proliferation.

If you don't have a wort chiller, you must employ other methods to bring down the temperature as fast as possible. One time-honored technique is to immerse the wort in a bathtub or large sink filled with cold water. Try to keep the lid on, and change the cold water frequently to conduct away as much heat as possible.

I take my hydrometer reading just as I fill the carboys because I want to know the extract degrees and therefore the potential alcohol.

I force the plastic blow-by tube into the neck of the carboy and put the other end into a bucket with about a gallon of sterilant (one tablespoon of chlorine into one gallon of water). This sterilant must always cover the end of the tube, and I change it every day the blow-by is in use.

A closed system has two incomparable advantages over the primary-secondary system. First, one needn't skim off the foamy layer of hops resins. Second, it saves a transfer of the wort from the primary to the secondary, avoiding the possibility of contamination.

Within four to six hours, the yeast has begun to work. Foam gathers on the surface, bringing brownish protein and hops particles with it to form a dark froth like dirty whipping cream.

In twenty-four hours the fermentation is in full cry, pushing froth up the tube. By the end of the second day the first bloom of fermentation has subsided. If I have filled the carboy to the top, I will have blown out two to six quarts of wort by then, depending upon the yeast and the temperature. In a few cases when I have simply added the wort to the lees of a previous batch, the fermentation may begin within an hour. I remember once putting the carboy in the bathroom rather than the basement (which was 20 degrees colder) and returning thirty minutes later to find foam pushing through the blow-by tube. I suspect the fermentation went so fast that time because the wort temperature was above 85° F. It was too hot.

In forty-eight to seventy-two hours, the insides of the tube and the exposed portion of the carboy walls are covered with resins. The remaining foam in the carboy is almost as clean as a hound's tooth.

From here, you have two options. You may let the beer finish fermenting in the same carboy with an airlock on top, or you may transfer the wort to another carboy, adding one to two quarts of water and an airlock. I have done both. I don't think it makes much difference, except that the insides of the carboy will be harder to clean if you allow the resins to harden on the glass.

In either case, I clothe the carboy and airlock in a black plastic toga to keep the light out. Since this batch is a lager, I carry the carboy to the coldest part of the basement, which in the winter is about 45°F.

Two or three days later, I add gelatin finings. I put one-half to one teaspoon of ordinary food gelatin in a saucepan with a cup of sterile water, let it soak for half an hour, then heat it gently to dissolve it (do not boil). I pour this into the wort, shake the carboy well to disperse the gelatin, and then forget about the batch for at least two weeks. I use the bubbler as a guide to the fermentation's progress. My rule of thumb is to wait until the frequency of bubbles has slowed to one every ninety seconds or longer. Usually this point comes within four weeks. Try as I might, the hydrometer reading will not drop below 1012–1016, let alone reach 1000 as some say it should. This is because there is a small amount of proteinous solids which always remain unfermented.

On bottling day, I assemble two cases of clean bottles, a clean siphoning hose and copper pick-up, and set to work. I don't usually sterilize my bottle caps. Leaving the yeast sediment behind, I transfer the beer into another clean carboy and add three-quarters to one cup dextrose and one-half teaspoon ascorbic acid dissolved in sterile water or heated beer.

You may want to try a poor man's kraeusening. Kraeusening is used by some lager brewers, notably Anheuser-Busch and Anchor Steam, and involves adding some young beer in the primary fermentation stage to aged beer about to be bottled. This produces a natural carbonation. Fred Eckhardt writes about this at length in his *Treatise on Lager Beers*. I have never tried it, preferring the simpler method of adding a packet of yeast to my priming sugar.

Assuming I haven't made any mistakes, this lager can be drunk in about three weeks, but it will be much better if I wait two to three months. The longer and colder the aging process, the better the beer. For me, the gratification of drinking lager increases in direct relation to the length of its deferral, up to five or six months. Since I have plenty of other brews coming to maturity during the interim, I am not concerned about the delay. I am content to place the two cases out of sight and forget about them—for a while. I confess that after a month of aging I often drink a bottle a week to see how it is coming along.

Some evening, when I am down in the cellar counting cases, I will just "happen" upon the lager and decide to try a bottle. I put it in the freezer for an hour to get its temperature down to the mid-40°s, knowing that it will still make its presence and bouquet known. I retrieve it, flip the cap, and pour a mug. I sniff it and check the color at arm's length against the light. I take a sip and shepherd the liquid around to all the taste buds I can find. The aroma curls out of my mouth and into my nose. All's right with the world.

("Professor Surfeit," a.k.a. Charlie Papazian, deals with home brewers' questions in *Zymurgy*, and in the Winter 1982 issue he answered en masse all the agonized queries about flat, sour, cidery, cloudy, moldy, overcarbonated beer. I can do no better than to direct you to his discussion of the single most nefarious, nasty, evil, heinous, odious, despicable cause of bad beer: bacterial infection.)

The more I brewed, the better the beer became. Yet I didn't like spending eight hours to make a batch of beer. Beer twice as good as extracts was not worth four times as many hours of preparation. There had to be a way either to shorten the brewing time or to increase the batch size. I didn't have the equipment to boil more than six gallons at a time, and I could think of no way to shave time from the mashing or sparging.

Then it struck me. Why not combine extracts and all-grain? Why not make a concentrate by adding six pounds of extract to the wort boil, double up on the hops, run the brew through the wort chiller, and then add cool water to make up ten gallons?

It worked. The first time I tried the new recipe, I called the batch Seven Sins Lager in honor of all my past brewing transgressions. In addition to the Ma Vlast recipe, I used a can of dark and a can of light malt extract, and doubled the hops. The result was a fine amber-colored lager. It was excellent.

Four cases for a day's work no longer seemed so onerous. The beer didn't taste quite as forceful as the all-grain, but it had more body than the all-extract variety. Ten gallons filled a keg, plus a case of bottles. What's more, I could keep enough on hand for all my friends by brewing every five to six weeks, rotating between lagers, ales, and stouts. With these ten-gallon batches, I had reached a certain brewing equilibrium.

My cost for a ten-gallon batch is as follows. I should note, however, that I get all my ingredients at the local food co-op, where prices are much lower than those at specialty shops.

2 cans of malt @ $4.00 apiece	$ 8.00
Hops	4.00
Yeast	1.50
10 pounds of grain @ 60 cents a pound	6.00
Hot water, chlorine, gypsum, etc.	.50
TOTAL	$20.00

This gives me a case for $5.00 or about 21 cents per bottle (excluding my labor).

A Busman's Holiday

One fall afternoon, the postman brought the usual load of political appeals, junk mail, three newspapers, and a few pieces of legitimate first-class mail. Almost lost among the flashy catalogues for tools and kitchenware was a brown package from Chris's sister, who was then studying in England. Inside was a paperback book entitled *The Good Beer Guide* published by the Campaign for Real Ale (CAMRA).

In language reminiscent of a nineteenth-century broadside, the *Guide* began:

> Ladies and Gentlemen of the Drinking Public. Once again the Campaign for Real Ale presents for your delectation almost 6,000 of the very Finest Hostelries in these Islands that dispense that great delight: Traditional Draft Beer. Members of the Campaign have spared no effort to seek out Sundry Inns, Taverns and Public Houses that keep and serve their Ale in the most Excellent of Condition.

Traditional draft beer or ale, the jacket cover continued, is brewed only from malted barley, water, hops, and yeast to make the bitters, milds, and porters. The means of dispensing are several—from the cask, the beer engine, or electric power—"but all these Systems eschew the Noisome Carbonic Gas which the Purveyors of Inferior Brew use to mask the Lackluster Taste of their Dubious Products."

Here were words to warm the heart of all brewing purists. I spent the evening with a pint of home-brewed porter, perusing the *Guide* as dreamily as a dedicated pub crawler might examine a map of London.

The *Guide* gave a brief history of the venerable English pub, telling how that institution was the outgrowth of hearty private hospitality. It also listed all of the nation's 170 operating breweries along with their addresses and telephone numbers.

Both Chris and I had been to England several times, and she had lived there for seven years—albeit before she reached drinking age. We liked the hearty English ales and stouts. Four years earlier, we had driven around southern Ireland and in twelve days managed to explore some forty-four bars and the bottoms of countless glasses of Guinness, Murphy's, and Smithwick's Ale. We were experienced, if not hardened, pub crawlers.

Why not make a vacation of visiting some of these small breweries listed in the CAMRA *Guide?* I had toured two breweries in this country, the Anheuser-Busch plant in Merrimack, New Hampshire (capacity 3 million barrels a year), and the world's largest brewery, Coors, in Golden, Colorado (15 million barrels). These were not breweries, they were factories—as impersonal and sterile and remote from good beer as giant bakeries are from homemade bread. The CAMRA *Guide* described small breweries producing as little as a hundred gallons per week.

We had friends in Oxfordshire who would find us a place to stay, and a quick look at the *Guide* revealed seven breweries within thirty miles of Stonesfield, our prospective base. We contacted our friends and dispatched letters to those seven breweries, asking if we could tour their establishments. We didn't expect any replies; we only hoped they would be hospitable when we arrived.

Before describing the breweries we visited, I should say something about the origins of CAMRA and English home brewing.

Imagine thousands of outraged housewives turned loose on Procter & Gamble and Lever Brothers, demanding that they make "real" soap. Imagine American beer drinkers picketing Schlitz to change the formulation of its beer. Imagine other beer lovers filing a friend-of-the-court brief against General Brewing Company's takeover of Pearl Brewing Co. With only modest exaggeration, this gives some idea of what beer historian Michael Jackson calls "the most successful consumer movement in history."

The spiritual ancestor of CAMRA was a beer-drinking club in Britain called The Society for the Preservation of Beers from the Wood.

This became the Campaign for the Revitalization of Ale and subsequently, in 1973, the present Campaign for Real Ale. The cause attracted a hodgepodge of beer lovers, food nuts, defenders of the English pub, traditionalists, small-is-beautiful advocates, and home brewers. Within five years, the Campaign had 20,000 members in 140 local chapters across Great Britain. Its members came from all socioeconomic classes, but the largest and most vociferous group consisted of young professionals.

CAMRA members united to fight twin devils: "concentration and pressurization." They claimed that traditional, living, cask-conditioned ale was being progressively destroyed by the business and brewing tactics of the so-called Big Six major brewing companies: Courage, Allied Breweries, Scottish & Newcastle, Watneys, Bass Charrington, and Whitbread. By 1970, the Big Six were producing over 80 percent of all the beer sold in Britain. Their relentless drive for economies of scale dictated that they sell fewer varieties to more people. This they did by building ever-larger "mega-keggeries" and shipping the beer by huge lorries throughout the country. The Big Six also followed the pattern of giant American breweries in formulating their brews for the lowest common denominator of taste.

A CAMRA member compared the mass-produced "keg beer" with "real ale" and found, "It is essentially the difference between real draft beer, a living product in which fermentation continues in the pub cellar, and filtered beer, which is sterile (all living yeast organisms having been removed) and which needs added carbon dioxide in order to recreate the 'lively' appearance of draft beer."

Not only were the Big Six pasteurizing and homogenizing ales, as their American cousins were doing, they were also introducing Continental-style lagers into their pubs. And this lighter, clearer, colder beverage was picking up an increasing market share. To the purists it was as if baseball had begun to cut into cricket's popularity. By the early 1980s, lager's market share was over 20 percent and climbing strongly.

The Big Six did not flourish simply by building larger beer factories. They acquired scores of small breweries and either shut them down or turned them to the production of Big Six brands. The effect of these buy-outs on customer choice was particularly stifling because of the British system of tied houses. Since the eighteenth century, most of the pubs in Britain have been owned by breweries. Over 80 percent of the pubs in 1980—that is, 60,000—were operated by the Big Six. Once they possessed these outlets, the breweries were naturally disinclined to sell beers other than their own.

From CAMRA's standpoint, an even worse sin occurred when a member of the Big Six bought and closed a smaller regional brewery and shut down the attached pubs as well. In hundreds of cases, this left villages without a center. As the president of one small brewery said, "A village that loses its pub starts to die. I would never want to be responsible for administering that kind of blow."

As an example of what could happen, Courage acquired a Bristol brewery in 1961. Between its own pubs and those of the formerly independent company, Courage suddenly controlled 64 percent of the drinking places in the city of Avon. An American might not care if Budweiser sold 64 percent of the beer in his town, but the English CAMRA members regarded it as a tragedy and an outrage.

They were convinced that, if unchecked, the industry concentration would eliminate all the real draft beer in the country. So they set themselves to patronizing and defending those smaller regional breweries that still made real ale. In addition, they filed a number of studies and reports with the government Price and Food Standards Commissions to show that smaller breweries offered better value, and castigated the Big Six for failing to offer information about their ingredients. As they marched to protest the closing of small breweries, they picked up reams of national publicity.

By the mid-1970s, to everyone's surprise, the Big Six were on the defensive. The Monopolies Commission took a more careful look at their takeover proposals. Several of the Big Six resurrected the names, if not the formulations, of breweries they had swallowed. What's more, they spent millions of pounds proclaiming their devotion to "real ale."

At about the same time, and no doubt spurred by CAMRA's success, a score of small breweries opened up, among them the first new brewery in London in fifty years. One traditional brewer said that the survival of many small regional beermakers might not have been possible without the support of the CAMRA movement.

Interestingly, a comparative study in Britain found that the local and regional breweries were significantly more profitable than the Big

Six, as long as they kept to the area they could best supply and serve. The majors were simply spread too thin. A significant factor in the success of small brewers was their production of "real ale."

Modern English home brewing dates from 1963, when Chancellor of the Exchequer Reginald Maudling lifted all restrictions on private brewing, provided none was sold. In a curious parallel to the American experience, British home brewing had been declining almost to oblivion since 1880. The reasons for it were quite different, however. In America, local breweries sprang up in so many communities that there was little aesthetic or financial incentive to compete at home. In Britain, however, many people brewed for distinctly economic reasons, and in 1880 the Gladstone government imposed a tax that made it cheaper for the poor (for whose benefit the tax was supposedly levied) to buy beer from the "common," or public, brewers than to make their own.

Home brewing grew rapidly in the 1960s under a combination of influences: rebellion against pasteurized keg beer, reduced choice in commercial beer, increase in leisure time, and the rising cost of beer in pubs, where 80 percent of British brews are consumed. Lacking good information and equipment, many home brewers weighed in heavily with the sugar. The resulting beers were cannon fodder for the cartoonists and wags of the day.

As the decade progressed, home brewers refined their taste and the malting companies responded with improved malts and hops. The companies began to produce kits with premixed hops and malt. Just add water, boil, cool, add yeast, and away you go. So popular were the kits that the nation's largest drugstore chain, Boots, became the largest retailer of home brewing supplies, garnering millions of pounds in sales per year. By 1980, an estimated 10 percent of the beer consumed in England was being made at home.

In England, a pint of beer in a pub is five to seven times more expensive than one brewed at home. No matter how much a fellow wants to hang out at his friendly "local," if he has limited funds and an unlimited thirst, he will inevitably turn to home brewing. By contrast, the cost differential between commercial American beer and decent home brew is closer to 2:1. British kits are convenient, simple, consistent, and . . . boring. English home brew supply shops offer a

range of malts, hops and yeasts, but the vast majority of their customers buy the same ingredients month-in and month-out because they
brew for financial, not aesthetic reasons.

Once settled in Stonesfield, a village of three hundred people, sur-
rounded by barley fields, we tried its three pubs. The nearest was a
Courage outlet, the Black Sheep, which was longer on boisterous dart-
contest atmosphere than on real ale. Then we headed for the two largest breweries on the list, Morrell's in Oxford and Morland's in Abing-
don. Morrell's annual production is 40,000 barrels, and Morland's is
70,000. (The English barrel is thirty-six gallons, compared to the
American barrel of thirty-one gallons.) Both head brewers had received our letters and gave us personally conducted tours.

By American standards, Morrell's and Morland's are tiny, about
one-twentieth the size of an average U.S. brewery, but compared to
my ten-gallon basement brewery, they were enormous. Thanks to my
home brewing experience, however, I found it easy and enjoyable to
follow the process from grinding through mashing, sparging, boiling,
and fermentation to kegging. At the end, the brewers served us some
of their products in employees' tap rooms. Both breweries were over
a hundred years old, but their equipment was relatively new and thus
lacked the architectural romance one associates with an old-fashioned
facility.

Tradition greeted us in spades at the Hook Norton Brewery about
thirty miles west of Oxford. Hook Norton is one of the few remaining
"tower breweries"—great, classic, five-story wooden structures built
in the late nineteenth century. Louvers in the Victorian cupola vented
the brew kettles' steam, and on this chill December morning, great
clouds wreathed the upper stories.

David Clarke, third-generation brewer and owner, led us through
the brewery from top to bottom, just as the grain, hops, and water
progress from the tower down to the basement casking operation. "We're
dragging ourselves into the nineteenth century," he quipped as he
showed us the 1890 steam engine and the 1920s "coppers," or boilers.
Only the white plastic fermenting vessels looked contemporary. In the
middle of the tour, Clarke paused for five minutes to help an employee
add Fuggles and Comet hops and a small amount of dark malt extract
to a brew. Then it was down into the basement, where, in a corner,

Clarke served us half-pints of his three ales. He drew the beer directly from wooden kegs placed there for the employees. They were all delicious, especially Old Hookey, a well-hopped, darker ale.

We next drove to the rolling Cotswold hills laced with sheep farms and fields of brussels sprouts and barley. In a small valley north of Stow-on-the-Wold, we found a brewery that gave new dimension to the word *idyllic*. In a series of connected stone buildings dating back to the fifteenth century, L. Claude Arkell brews twenty barrels of pale ale daily for his seventeen tied houses and inns. The brewery stands beside a trout pond whose denizens feed on some of the spent grains, while above them float stately black swans, geese, and ducks. Water from the pond turns a mill wheel that is connected to Arkell's grain grinder. Twenty years ago, Arkell harvested his own barley, malted it in one part of the barn, and used the product in his beer. Now he buys the barley locally. Hops come from nearby Worcestershire.

He seemed so devoted to his brewery and so matter-of-fact about its operation that we asked what it would take to start a brewery from scratch and operate it profitably.

"It wouldn't be so hard," Arkell said. "I never went to brewing school. I learned from other brewers, picked their brains, kept my mouth shut. Good brewing is really only four things: get your water chemistry right, watch your brewing temperature, clean the pipes, and use your noddle." He surely made it seem simple and straightforward. What a life—to build a brewery by a trout pond, raise sheep and fruit trees on the hillside, feed the geese and swans at dusk.

Arkell said he spends as much time as he can with other brewers because he feels he can always learn more. One of them had recently introduced him to some new hops pellets that Arkell now used most of the time.

"You know, the big brewers could crush me in a second," he said. "But they won't because the influence of CAMRA has made them shy of public censure. I am worried about the growth of home brewing kits because they aren't taxed. Taxes are what make beer so expensive in the pub.

"I'm a third-generation brewer. If you want to see someone who started from scratch, visit Tom Litt. He buys yeast from me once a week."

Litt was already on our list, so we headed for the village of South Leigh, home of the Mason Arms. We had been intrigued with CAMRA's description of Litt's pub as a "home brewery." There, behind the bar, across from a warm oak log fire, we found him engaged in a lively discussion with a customer. They were talking about the Celebration Ale that Litt had brewed to commemorate the marriage of Prince Charles and Lady Diana.

Litt remembered our letter and invited us to come back in the morning. "In the meantime, these are on the house," he said. He handed each of us a pint of Sowlye (South Leigh) Ale, his one and only brew. It was a fine beer, malty yet hopped enough to be memorable.

When we arrived the next morning, we could see the steam rising from a former stable behind the inn. We found Litt stoking an ancient, rusty, coal-fired boiler. As he scampered between the boiler room, brew house and "cellar" (an enclosed horse stall), he told us how he came to brew.

A farmer's son, Litt had bought the run-down farmhouse in 1964, converted it to an inn, and added a restaurant that was good enough to draw people out of Oxford for luncheon. This success made him restless for more challenge, and in 1974, on a half-serious bet, he assembled some equipment and brewed a seventy-five-gallon batch of beer, which, his surprised friends had to agree, was good. Over the next twelve months, he refined both equipment and recipe until he was satisfied. Only one vessel, the hundred-gallon boiling kettle, was built to order. The rest was surplus equipment: a potato cooker from the army, coolers from a dairy, used kegs from other breweries, and a thirty-year-old coal-fired steam boiler. His total investment was less than $10,000.

Tom Litt exuded enthusiasm and pragmatism. He nursed the boiler as if it were human. He used no special water treatment. His conditioning room, where the beer ages in kegs for six to twelve days, was simply an enclosed and cooled horse stall. When the beer was ready to drink, he rolled the keg across the parking lot and tapped it in a room behind his simple bar.

"There's no mystery in brewing. Just keep the place clean. The trouble with most brewers is that they are never satisfied. They are always trying to change this ingredient or that procedure."

"Do you have any problem with health inspectors?" I asked.

"None at all. They know that if I don't keep the brewery clean, the beer will spoil and people won't buy it." As for the tax collector, the district officer had a key to the stable and he could and did come in at odd hours to check the correlation between the ingredients Litt buys and the amount of beer he sells.

As we watched, Litt climbed a ladder with a five-gallon plastic bucket and emptied its dark syrupy contents into the boiler.

"What's that?" I asked.

"Malt extract."

"Malt extract!" I gasped. "You mean you don't mash?"

"Of course not. Why should I? I can make perfectly good beer with the extracts and save time and trouble and expense."

I reeled at the simplicity of it all. Unless I had a tin tongue, he was making an extract ale fully as good as any mashed version I could produce. What was he doing right, and what was I doing wrong?

As he puttered around the brewery, Litt dictated the recipe for his Sowlye Ale (O.G. 1037):

100 gals. water	3 lbs. liquid yeast from Arkell
100 lbs. Edme liquid	1 pint finings at kegging time
Malt Extract	Handful of loose Goldings for
3 lbs. Golding hops	finishing hops at the end

Boil for an hour, cool it down using a dairy cooler, pump it into the primary fermenter for 4 days, then into kegs for about 10 days and it's ready to drink.

Was it the wooden kegs he used that made the beer so good? No, they were lined with stainless steel and gave off no special taste. Was it Litt's careful handling? He was no more careful than I was. Was I exaggerating the ambience of South Leigh, Oxfordshire? Perhaps. But that still did not explain it all. How he made such good beer so simply gnawed at me for the rest of our stay in England.

The key to Litt's financial success lay in his reliance on the brewery for only a portion, in his case roughly one-third, of his income. The inn and restaurant provided the other two-thirds. It would be impossible, he said, to make a living from the brewery alone. Nor would he want to. Litt was quite happy to spend only one day a week brewing enough beer to sell in the following week. His seemed a very civilized existence.

Fifty miles away in London, David Bruce was anything but content with a hundred gallons a week. Bruce is the founder of five brew pubs, four in London and one in Bristol. His menagerie of pubs are named The Fox and Firkin, Goose and Firkin, Frog and Firkin, etc. A former manager at Courage's and Theakston's (a small Yorkshire brewery), Bruce took a third mortgage on his London house to launch the first Firkin and in four years was grossing $4 million annually.

By the time Bruce got to London in 1978, there were only four brew pubs extant in England, one of them in the city. Bruce believed that the public was ready for a new round of brew pubs if done with flair. He bought old, mostly run-down pubs and put breweries in the cellars. One pub featured a porthole, another a glass section in the floor through which customers could watch the beer being brewed. Bruce sold beers with such arresting names as Dogbolter, Earthstopper, and Sphincter Special. He produced T-shirts and buttons and formed clubs of regular drinkers. In short, "We're a marketing organization as much as a production organization," said the chief lieutenant, Andy MacDonald.

When we told him that the visit to South Leigh had aroused our interest in tiny commercial brewing, Bruce told us to drive down to Ringwood near the English Channel and see the brewery there. "They've made beer for us when we've run short. What's more, they are selling whole brewery kits—plans, equipment, and all. They even take on students."

The Ringwood Brewery was located in a couple of unpretentious stucco buildings on a back street. The mash tun and boiler with their wooden insulating jackets looked more like hot tubs than brewing vessels. The kegging operation brought to mind the disarray of a bus company repair shop. Ringwood brews its own beer and distributes it to the free trade (nontied houses) nearby, but its bread and butter has been selling the plans and, when possible, the actual equipment for micro-breweries across Great Britain. The cost was roughly $40,000 for plans and equipment for a brewery with a capacity of ten to fifteen barrels. When we visited Ringwood, they had sold about a dozen brewery kits.

Two other factors made the trip to Ringwood worthwhile. It was the first time we had heard of beer sold right out of the brewery. Customers brought their own jugs or purchased them from the brewery and took them home full of porter, bitter, Forty-Niner, or Old Thumper. This retail share of the business had risen to 25 percent in just one year. Ringwood's ales were respectable, but not as good as Hook Norton's or Arkell's.

The second discovery at Ringwood was the name of an American who had served an apprenticeship there. He was William Newman, of Albany, New York, who had fallen in love with English ale and decided to build a brewery in the United States. In 1979 he had worked at Ringwood for four months and then bought the plans for his own operation. The vision of an American single-handedly proposing to blow foam literally and figuratively in the face of the American giants was most intriguing. We would go see him when we returned home.

"Many Are Called . . ."

In the first months after we returned from Britain, I read a number of articles about small breweries in the United States. Almost every issue of *Zymurgy* and *Brewers Digest* included information about a "micro-brewery" in California or Colorado or Oregon. These new breweries produced from several hundred to perhaps 1,200 barrels a year, except for Anchor Brewing Co. in San Francisco, which sold about 25,000 barrels of the incomparable Anchor Steam and Anchor Porter annually. All the micro-breweries in the country together produced less annually than Budweiser (annual 1982 production: 59 million barrels) did in one day. In contrast to the hundreds and thousands of employees at the big breweries, the micros were often one- and two-person shops founded by former home brewers who were longer on love and ingenuity than money. But the articles painted pictures of near-universal success. Reporters for newspapers, magazines, and television gave the brewers free and unquestioning publicity. "We're selling all we can make" was a recurrent comment from the micro-brewers.

There is a bit of the host in all of us. I've often dreamed about running a restaurant that served meals made memorable by my beer. I would have to divide my time between the cellar and the main dining room, overseeing the brewing and squiring the guests. Why not build a glass wall or floor as David Bruce had done in London, and let the customers see me making the week's ale, stout, or lager?

This fantasy took me back eighty years to Montana where my grandfather and his brother established Central Park on the outskirts of Helena, the state capital. The park contained baseball fields, a bandstand, a small zoo, and a beer garden which served schooners and kegs of lager from the nearby Horsky and Kessler breweries. I would go one step further and offer my own.

During the next months, I offered more and more beer to both friends and strangers. To those who liked it, I asked, Would you ever pay money for this? How much? What kind of container would you like to see? How important is the label and the advertising? In a way, I had been testing the market almost as long as I had been brewing, from the first offerings of Prohibition Pilsner, when most of it was left under the chairs or poured into the plants, to recent times when people asked for it unsolicited.

Wouldn't the public respond enthusiastically to a beer made in Vermont with its image of purity, hard work, and virtue? What about the tourists and the out-of-state students who flock down the slopes and hills to the bars every night? Make an intriguing enough label and they would take it home to New York and Boston as a collector's item.

About this time, my brother sent me an article from *Beverage World,* a packaging-industry trade journal. Under the title "The Bell Doesn't Toll for All Small Brewers," Harold O. Davidson voiced unexpected optimism about the future of small breweries. In contrast to the general expectation of further concentration within the industry, Davidson pointed to a limit on economies of scale. Beyond a certain figure, it would become too expensive to transport a product of 96 percent water. This limit provided an opening for the small and regional brewers. Citing a study by the Stanford Research Institute, Davidson foresaw a "micro-segmentation" within the industry. The market would split into specialized sectors and progressively subdivide as an increased percentage of the population followed more individualistic buying patterns. This article encouraged me to think that small breweries might have a chance, depending upon how and where they marketed their product.

It was time to stop dreaming and visit William Newman's brewery in Albany, New York.

In a weedy, seedy, industrial area a mile from downtown Albany, Chris and I found the William S. Newman Brewing Company, Inc. Only a bright new green-and-white sign announcing BREWERY distinguished the building from half a dozen other run-down brick ware-houses nearby. The structure had been a mattress factory until thirty years earlier when fire had gutted its innards, leaving it abandoned until Newman bought it.

A tall, lean, intense man in tie, sweater, heavy trousers, and rub-ber boots introduced himself as William Newman. A former news-paper editor, teacher, laborer, and budget analyst for the state of New York, he was hospitable in a reserved way. He explained that he had to make some beer deliveries that morning and turned us over to his assistant brewer, Mark Harder, who had a Ph.D. in biochemistry and two years of home brewing experience.

The front door opened into an area with a jerry-rigged bar in one corner and the entrance to a small office in another. Here the brewery sold beer straight from the keg in plastic containers, just as Ringwood does. The containers were supposed to be reusable, and customers were expected to rinse them out and return for more beer. This business already accounted for a third of Newman's sales.

The next room explained why Newman called his brewery Ring-wood West. His boiling vessel, hop separator, and four 1,000-gallon fermenters were carbon copies of the Ringwood equipment. All the walls were newly painted and insulated.

The largest room in the 10,000-square-foot building provided space for grain storage and grinding, a 600-gallon mash tun, and keg wash-ing and filling equipment. Harder explained that the brewery worked on a two-day brewing cycle because the boiling kettles only held half of what was mashed. Total production time from grinding grain to tapping a keg at a bar was two and a half weeks. They were making a Pale Ale using Ringwood's recipe and yeast. Barley was domestic, while hops were a mixture of domestic, English, and German, delivered in two-hundred-pound burlap-wrapped "pockets." We saw six of them standing like patient draft horses waiting their turn.

Midway through the tour, Newman returned to join us. The in-spiration for his brewery, he explained, was a newspaper article he'd read in London while he and his wife were vacationing there in 1978. It described the opening of the first London pub brewery in half a century.

He returned to this country and visited such small breweries as

Anchor and D. G. Yuengling & Sons in Pottsville, Pennsylvania. He took a two-week course in brewing at one of the three American brewing schools, the U.S. Brewers Academy. One classmate, an executive at Molson in Newfoundland, told Newman that if he were twenty years younger, he, too, would open a small brewery.

Newman went to England again and served a four-month apprenticeship at Ringwood. When he got back to Albany, he spent half a year assembling his construction and financing package. His biggest problem was not raising the money or formulating the brew, but finding a suitable location. His first choice in a light industrial zone was next to a Fundamentalist church. The congregation was not pleased by the prospect of having a brewery next door and successfully opposed his permit application. After he found the mattress factory, he put together $250,000 which included 15 percent of his own money with the remainder from a local bank and city and state development loans.

Newman chose to keg his entire production. "It's cheaper and simpler," he said. "I'm surprised that other small breweries are bottling. When you bottle, you have to buy all the containers, and they disappear faster than the kegs. You need bottle soakers, fillers, crowners, and labelers. And the time involved! I think the largest part of production time is in filling the bottles. Where do you get small-scale bottling equipment? And then how do you maintain it?"

He said that the Albany area had a higher than average draft beer consumption rate, and this would help make his beer a local favorite. He expected to have about 150 outlets out of the 1,600 bars in the four-county area. He had 14 when we visited him. Since his beer tasted best at around 50° F., he insisted that the bars serve it at that temperature. If they didn't have a cooler capable of keeping the beer at that temperature, they would have to buy a specially built one that could do the job. Furthermore, they had to wait at least twelve hours before serving the beer once it was delivered so that the yeast could have a chance to settle. Newman claimed that all his customers complied with these rules.

What would happen if he sold a bad batch? Newman said he didn't ever plan to sell bad beer. He had worked hard to arrive at a formula that pleased him and should please the customer. He had made thirteen batches before he was satisfied. He was confident that Albany

drinkers were ready for English-style ale served at English temperatures. The slight cloudiness and the sediment would be marks of distinction.

We went next door to the Thatcher Street Pub, a workingman's
bar and one of his best customers, Newman said. We sat down and
ordered hamburgers while Newman fetched a fistful of steins and sat
down opposite us. We raised glasses and my mind suddenly flashed
back to the first time I had offered my best beer to friends. I had been
studiously offhand, but I had churned inside. Bill Newman looked the
same way. What should we say? Suppose the beer was terrible. I began dredging my vocabulary for words of comfort and praise.

I took a sip. Whew! I brightened. It tasted like . . . Ringwood's
Forty-Niner. "Tasty," I said, and Newman relaxed. It was very much
akin to other traditional ales we drank in England, but I wondered
how it would sell in American Lagerland. How long would it take for
Albany palates to adjust to the taste, appearance, and temperature of
Newman's Pale Ale? Newman obviously hoped it would happen before he ran out of money. One precedent offered hope—yoghurt had
caught on in the land of cottage cheese.

My next step was to call the executive secretary of the Brewers
Association of America, the trade organization for smaller breweries.
William O'Shea, a lawyer and brewery advocate by profession, had
run the association for over forty years. He knew everyone in the industry. Nicknamed Mr. Small Brewery, he was also known as the "industry's undertaker" because he had watched the demise of hundreds
of American breweries. I thought he would be sympathetic to my questions about starting a small brewery.

If he was, he expressed it in an odd way. When I outlined my
fantasy, he said bluntly, "You're crazy. People come in here or call
every week with the idea of building a small brewery and they don't
have a clue as to how tough a market this is." He went on in this vein
for abut ten minutes and then abruptly announced that he had work
to do.

He dismissed most of the micro-brewers, or "boutique brewers,"
as hobbyists who would do little to help the industry. He conceded
that one of the small new breweries might succeed. "This fellow
McAuliffe of New Albion Brewery in California has the right attitude

and the necessary mechanical skills to do it himself. He built all his own equipment."

"What about Fritz Maytag of Anchor Brewing?" I asked.

"Oh, he's a special case. He knew what he was doing from the beginning."

No one likes to be called a fool, and I smarted from his criticism. But later, after talking to several small brewers, I realized that I had been mistaken in my judgment of him. These men liked O'Shea and said he had been a determined and resourceful defender of local and regional breweries. His reserve and bluntness bespoke a deep awareness of the difficulties involved.

O'Shea did give me one thing besides a cold shower; he confirmed my sense that Maytag and McAuliffe were the godfathers of the microbrewing movement. Anyone at all serious about building a small brewery should visit them.

I had drunk Anchor Steam only four or five times, but each sip had been memorable. The beer was fully malted, honestly hopped, with an aftertaste as evocative as Guinness or Pilsner Urquell. Indeed, I put it on the same pedestal as these giants. Of McAuliffe's beer I knew nothing.

The Anchor Brewing Company is housed in a cream-colored former coffee factory in a mixed light industrial and residential neighborhood of San Francisco. You climb a flight of stairs to the office and find yourself looking directly onto the brewing floor. Across from the two office desks through a glass partition gleam the cones and chimneys of three copper vessels. Through another glass wall is the tap room, whose walls are festooned with old brewing advertising signs, photographs of steam beer breweries, and glass cases of brewing instruments and utensils. A carved oak bar serves beer to visitors and coffee or tea to employees.

One whole corner is devoted to souvenirs, such as belt buckles, T-shirts, aprons, and visors, all bearing the attractive red, blue, green, tan, and white emblem of "Anchor Steam Beer—Made in San Francisco since 1896."

I was shown into a room where a man was on his hands and knees, as intent as a child shooting marbles. He was flipping a two-inch-thick stack of three-by-four-foot sheets of bottle labels. In his well-tailored clothes, he looked more like a Boston investment banker than a brewer. But behind the rimless hexagonal glasses, his eyes were restless, quizzical, and determined. Speaking almost to himself, he said he must decide in twenty-four hours whether the printer should proceed with these eight million labels, which was a year's supply. "Do you realize how many eight million bottles are?" he asked. He was thinking out loud. The blue in the label still did not quite match the blue in the bottle cap: "The color is drifting too much." He wanted them just right. He gave word to have the printer try one more match.

"Now, what can I do for you?" Fritz Maytag asked.

I said I was one more home brewing moth drawn to the light of commercial brewing and I had come to learn how he'd made Anchor such a successful company.

We sat down at a table where I could look out onto the copper brewing kettles and he told me his story.

In 1965, Fritz Maytag, heir to the washing machine fortune, with a degree in Asian Studies from Stanford, was, as he put it, "drifting." He had helped start a dairy business and winery in Chile, and he didn't want to go back to the family trade in Iowa. During a visit to San Francisco, he went to dinner at one of his college haunts, the Spaghetti Factory, where as a student he had drunk schooners of Anchor Steam Beer, a local brew and the last of a great tradition of steam beers.

Steam beer is to beer what the banjo is to musical instruments— America's only genuine contribution to the field. The name is derived from the strong carbonation in the beer when it ferments. It is a hybrid beverage first brewed during the Gold Rush days in the mid-nineteenth century, using lager yeast but at warmer ale-fermenting temperatures. The brewers also included the German-Bohemian system of kraeusening—adding some young beer to the aging beer to give it natural carbonation. When kegs of steam beer were tapped, they hissed and foamed in a manner unlike English-style ales. Spectators to the tapping applied the misnomer *steam* to the beer. California then had little or no ice or deep cellars in which to keep the beer cool. At one time, there had been twenty-seven steam beer breweries in San Francisco. By Prohibition this number had fallen to seven, and by

1965 there was only Anchor, producing less than five hundred barrels a year.

At the Spaghetti Factory, Maytag heard that Anchor was for sale. The next day he visited the brewery and, on an impulse, bought it lock, stock, and lauter tun.

"It was a crazy thing to do. The brewery was a disaster. The equipment was ghastly. The quality was inconsistent. When it was good, it was very good. At its worst, it was pretty bad. Some of the bad beer was getting into the trade and making a poor sales situation worse. They made a batch about every two months. They didn't even boil the wort; they just sort of simmered it. They sold only draft and the kegs were dirty and leaked."

At first, Maytag simply paid the bills and tried to halt the sales decline. But then he decided he either had to get out or get into the business all the way and make a going concern of it. "I was determined to see this brewery succeed as a real business. I wanted to sell beer at a reasonable price. I wanted to make a real beer, not a gimmick or a joke or a hype.

"I can't say that I bought the brewery with a lot of philosophical intent. It's true that from the first I was infatuated with the mystery of brewing, its alchemical aspects. There is something magical in our culture about the idea of alcohol and mind-altering substances that is moderately accepted. It is a dreadful thing in many ways. A lot of people have been killed by alcohol. Scary stuff. But I think it does a lot more good than harm. Beer is the common man's alcohol. Breweries are places where you literally create beer out of grain—it's really alchemy—turning grain into bubbly, sparkling, magic stuff that affects your attitude—makes you sing songs . . . and cry.

"Setting out to make a high-quality product was my theme from the beginning. I wanted a sense of security about the product because of the way it was made, the methods, equipment, etc. I wanted an old-fashioned, interesting, unusual way of brewing, a story I could talk about. I took what little we had at the brewery and what I could learn about this funny West Coast tradition of steam beer and cast a Platonic ideal of what Anchor Steam beer would be like if you had all the technology to make it simple and pure."

But to make it pure wasn't so simple. "It took years of building and testing, lots of money on rent and salaries to develop the beer and then sell it as a great local product."

Maytag took a number of brewing courses, but for the most part he taught himself on the job and through reading. He worked on the equipment. He made sure of what was needed and then spent the money to get it—stainless steel and copper everywhere. He received help from people in the dairy industry who had long experience with sanitation.

"We're doing something very weird, which is making beer at warm temperatures—fifties and sixties and holding it for a month. Sanitation must be our main concern. No brewery can be dirty and make good beer. There are very few organisms which grow in beer, but boy do they grow! The way we are doing it, we're asking for trouble—it's like leaving the apple pie to cool on the back porch for a week."

The vessels in which primary fermentation occurs are unique to brewing, being twenty-by-thirty-foot stainless-steel open pans, two and a half feet deep at one end and three and a half feet deep at the other.

It took Maytag five years to build up his sales from 500 to 1,200 barrels annually. In another three years he reached 7,000 and the company moved into the black for the first time. He began distributing in the western states, Minnesota, and New Jersey. Anchor was becoming a cult beer. He added an Anchor Porter and pushed the old brewery to its limit of 12,000 barrels.

In 1977 Maytag bought a used German brewhouse with a capacity of 40,000 barrels. He had it shipped to a new, larger building in San Francisco. In a couple of years, he was producing 18,000 barrels to break even, and by 1982, Anchor was distributing 28,500 barrels of steam and porter to twenty states. This is still less than one-thousandth of Budweiser's annual production, but then Maytag is assuredly not competing with Budweiser. Anchor is a strong, all-malt brew with four times the hops of the average American beer.

When I told him of my brewery fantasy, Maytag laughed and said scores of people had come to see him with the same dream.

"I try to talk to them all. I tell them that first it takes a lot of money. Industry estimates are a hundred to two hundred dollars per barrel of capacity installed. I think you have to look on the high side of that figure. I could never have done this without inherited money because no one would lend me the funds. I don't care how charming I was or how good the beer tasted. This is a risky business. The whole country, the whole world, is fully of empty breweries.

"Secondly, you need at least one person who will devote unbelievable effort to making good beer. Even so, it takes a lot of luck and a lot of talent because you can't make a good reputation quickly for a product unless you're very lucky.

"When I took over this brewery, there were only a few imports here, mainly Dos Equis, Guinness, and Heineken. The wine and cheese renaissances hadn't yet taken place, the greening of America was still to come, the whole 'good life' movement hadn't occurred. Americans didn't know yet that they were going to start to enjoy food and drink and savor quality and natural things.

"Beer is just beer. That's part of the problem and part of the fun of it. Wine is anything you want to make of it, but beer is beer. That's one reason I like making beer. On the one hand, it's the common man's drink. Nobody will pay a dollar a bottle for any great quantity of it. On the other hand, it's much harder to make than wine, takes more art and science. The biggest difference from wine is that beer lacks what I call the participation and risks of nature. Classic wine is made from grapes in one location. In good years they're great and in bad years they're bad. When you drink that wine, you participate in that risk.

"To build a successful brewery, you needn't spend as much money as I did, but you do have to sell your product, and that's something home brewers don't realize. We put in a lot of hours, years, selling here and then moving to Wyoming, Arizona, Boston, and Florida. In the whole Bay area we sell maybe two thousand barrels. The reason we range so far is that we can't sell enough here. The beer doesn't sell itself."

Maytag did not spend a lot of money on advertising, certainly nothing to compete with the majors. Instead, he assiduously cultivated opinion makers, newspaper writers, and the public through guided brewery tours. He made sure Anchor was entered in beer tastings around California. Anchor's reputation spread as beer lovers learned about the funny little dark "steam" beer that held its own against the more heavily advertised European imports.

Probably the most important lesson Maytag learned from all his reading and experimentation was to have near operating-room cleanliness in his brewhouse. The average visitor looks at the shining brew kettles through the window of the hospitality room, then turns to drink some beer. The alert home brewer will notice the fanatical maintenance. Maytag went first class on his equipment, not because he wanted to impress people but because of the need for sanitation. "Home brewers don't have this kind of problem. They brew maybe once a week, then put their equipment away until the next batch. If you take a shower once a week you can have a pretty decrepit shower stall, even a wooden one with a canvas floor. After using it on Saturday night it would be dry by Monday. Mold wouldn't grow and rot it. But take three showers a day every day, and that shower would literally walk away after a year. In a commercial brewery everything is wet and unless you clean well every day, you pick up mold and bacteria and wild yeast."

Maytag's polite demeanor turns scornful when he talks about people who think of brewing more as an art than a science.

"Let me tell you my dirty thumbprint theory. A group of people go to a little, seedy, dirty Mexican restaurant with fantastic tacos and tortillas. Back in the kitchen, there's the mama making tortillas. But they notice that her hands are dirty. They then conclude that the tortillas are good because they're made by a real woman who is kind of sloppy. Well, I don't buy it. The tortillas are good because the flour is the best or because the warmth of her hand provides the best temperature. It is not because of the dirt."

About sixty miles from Maytag's relatively splendid brewery, down a dusty road two miles from Sonoma, I found the New Albion Brewing Company in half of a metal twenty-by-forty-foot warehouse. I had to look hard because there was no sign except for a square hand-lettered board nailed to a piece of rusting machinery.

Jack McAuliffe had been a navy enlisted man based at a submarine base in northern Scotland in the 1960s when he discovered ale. When he ran short of money to spend at the pubs, he found a home brew shop nearby where he could buy his own ingredients. By the time he left the navy, McAuliffe had decided to build his own small brewery. This idea germinated during eight or nine years of odd jobs, including one as an optical engineer in Silicon Valley. McAuliffe may have lacked Maytag's money, but he shared his abiding desire to operate a commercially successful brewery.

In one way or another, every fantasizing micro-brewer in this country in the last decade or so has made this same dual pilgrimage, and consciously modeled himself on one or both of these two brewers. There is admiration for Maytag's systematic, conscientious reconstruction of the dying Anchor Brewing Co., and envy for the financial resources that allowed him to buy the best equipment.

There is also admiration for the perseverance, ingenuity, and outright brass of McAuliffe, the lonely, poor, dedicated junk rat and entrepreneur who through force of will designed and hand-built his little New Albion brewery. McAuliffe used every mechanical talent he had picked up since high school and then taught himself new skills as required.

McAuliffe is as different from Maytag as a bulldog is from a greyhound. Where Maytag chooses his words carefully, McAuliffe spits his out brusquely. Where Maytag operates an immaculate four-story building in San Francisco, McAuliffe oversees an operation that reflects his shade-tree mechanical skills. He constructed the brewery around government surplus fifty-five-gallon stainless-steel drums. Every piece of equipment, except for a surplus bottle washer (which he bought for $150), was fabricated by McAuliffe himself, including a malt hopper, all the fermentation tanks, and the boiler. The grinding mill he built from scratch, using a design from an 1852 brewing text. He trucked in his brewing water every two weeks from a secret spring in the hills above Sonoma. With that water he brewed between five and ten barrels a week.

The office of the New Albion Brewing Co. was as unprepossessing as the brewer. In one corner of the ten-foot-square room was an enormous safe, inside of which were a dozen brewing texts. Another corner contained boxes of advertising promotion materials, T-shirts, placards, and tabletop displays. The rest of the room was given over to a huge desk piled high with papers and two reclining kittens. Above the desk was a row of technical manuals, accounting and management texts.

McAuliffe chose the name New Albion for his beers because that was what Sir Francis Drake called the San Francisco Bay area when he stopped there on his circumnavigation of the world in 1589. Drake's ship, the *Golden Hinde*, continues its voyage on New Albion labels.

Most home brewers probably identify with McAuliffe more readily than with Maytag. McAuliffe is as proud as the next man and happy for the fame, but praise as emulation vexes him.

"People come in and say, 'If McAuliffe can do it, so can I,' so there's a lot of competitive pressure. I think it would be a wonderful thing to do a brewery in Vermont, but I wish people out here would leave me alone. This is my damn hill country!"

Just before driving out to see New Albion, I stopped at a local liquor store and asked the salesman about McAuliffe's beer. He said it had been selling well, particularly since he'd dropped the price by about 25 cents to 89 cents a bottle. He also said that McAuliffe had been distributing the beer himself.

McAuliffe explained that he'd originally gone through the traditional distribution system. "However, our beer doesn't have the shelf life or the volume of the larger breweries. Beer distributors are the same as distributors in any business. They have no interest in the product per se. The only thing that interests them is how much money they are making. So if you have a product that's delicate, different, high class, low volume, you get pushed over into the corner. And then when someone on their route wants it, they look around and bring some out that's been sitting in the worst possible conditions. It doesn't taste good and everyone steps on it because it isn't a high turnover item. So we just cut the Gordian knot and went directly to our local retail customers. Want a beer?"

Without waiting for an answer, he fetched two glasses and drew them full from a tap fitted into the wall between his bottling and fermentation rooms. It was mellow, a bit cloudy, and stronger than Newman's Pale Ale. It combined the colder temperature and carbonation expected in America with the full body and aroma of genuine English ale.

"How did you begin?" I asked.

"Well, you're a home brewer. You know how it is when your buddies suck down a couple of your brews and say, 'Jesus, wouldn't it be wonderful to do this for a living?' A brewery is a natural consequence of making beer.

"I've always liked the flow of water, playing in creeks as a kid, and I'm mechanical by nature. Unless you're wealthy beyond the dreams of avarice, you must have mechanical ability. Even if you are rich, money is not enough. One of the things I like to say is that farmers make wine and engineers make beer. You must like water and pumps and numbers. Sanitation is numero uno.

"Many people think there's an unlimited demand for this product. That's not true. We make a specialty beer, strongly flavored, more beery than most. It's difficult to sell. To sell your beer in a bar, you have to have one which is not only good but which elbows the other guys aside. Successful brewers play hardball; it's a mighty competitive business. It's the fast track.

"To run a micro-brewery you need the technical skills to brew the beer and get it out the door. Then you have to have all the financial knowledge and business skills of running any small business. Brewing is first and foremost a business."

What, I asked, did he see in the future of micro-breweries in this country?

"There are two areas—the image and the reality: what people think and the reality of the numbers and money. As the industry continues to shrink, the products you make have to become more and more alike in taste. You want to offend as few people as possible. When you own a large brewery, you can't afford to make a specialty beer. In that sense, there is more and more opportunity for the small, specialty brewer. In this country there is a choice of brands but no choice of style. People are becoming more interested in food that tastes different and a broadened taste will support more specialty beers. At the same time it will become increasingly difficult for these new beers to find a place on retail shelves. That's because parallel with the shrinkage in brewing companies comes a declining number of distributors. And most of them don't want to mess with thousand-barrel breweries."

I told him of all the home brewers I knew who were fascinated with building and running their own breweries, myself among them.

McAuliffe paused and gave me a long, knowing look laced with irony and said, "Many are called. That's for sure. How many will be chosen is another matter."

McAuliffe had recently concluded that a brewery New Albion's size was not viable, and he was scouring the financial countryside to find backing to triple the size of his operation. With the cost of money over 20 percent, he was afraid he might fail. But he had no reservation about whether he would do it all over again.

"First off, I like beer. Second, where else could I pick the bottles, pick the labels, choose the recipe, decide who will work for me, who will interview me? Where else could I have kittens on the desk?"

I left New Albion with a couple of brewery T-shirts and a bottle of beer. Jack McAuliffe had done what many home brewers dream of. He was the home brewer down the street who turned pro. He inspired us all. Still, the mote in my mind's eye was whether he could survive. Could he raise the money needed to expand? In seven years he never produced more than 350 barrels a year. That was despite tens of thousands of dollars of free publicity, early entry into the market and, from all I had heard, an excellent if sometimes inconsistent product. It was something to ponder.

"Why would a successful thirty-one-year-old executive with a major corporation risk his life savings on a project that almost guarantees he'll never be rich?" asked a press release. Because, in reply to its own question, Matthew P. Reich had a mission to "bring a distinctive, flavorful, American beer to the American market."

The release went on to tell the story of this Bronx-born, summa cum laude graduate of the University of Massachusetts, Citicorp leasing officer, Hearst Corporation executive, and wine expert who discovered he wanted to spend his life selling beer.

I had heard rumors that Reich had wanted to build the first new commercial brewery in New York City in fifty years. Then I opened a copy of *The New Yorker* and found an article about him. Reich's public relations firm was not malingering, I thought.

I went down to New York City to see him. At first estimate, Reich thought he could build a brewery for about $1 million. When he found he could raise no more than a quarter of that, one of his investors suggested that he subcontract the beermaking to an existing brewery. Then he would be free to concentrate on the marketing. "I had seen the kinds of bacterial infection other micro-brewers were having. I didn't want that. Even big brewers with all the controls sometimes have those problems."

Reich convinced Joseph Owades, a brewing industry consultant and director of the Center for Brewing Studies in Boston to help him formulate the brew. The two went to F. X. Matt, the president of the West End Brewing Co. in Utica, New York, with their proposal. Matt listened to Owades's presentation and agreed to produce five hundred-barrel batches of the beer that Reich and Owades designed.

This was the origin of New Amsterdam Amber Beer, an all-malt lager made with 80 percent pale and 20 percent crystal malt and fresh Cascade and Hallertau hops. It is fermented at the relatively high temperature of 65° F., so it is a variation on steam beer, but made in enclosed fermenters.

Reich's market research told him to aim for two male markets, the eighteen- to twenty-four-year-old college crowd and the twenty-four- to forty-year-old young professional who drank imported beer for status and flavor. His "connoisseur's beer" is sold in single bottles only in delicatessens where the customers are "insensitive" to prices of 95 cents to $1.40 per twelve-ounce bottle, and in saloons where bottles can cost as much as $3.00 each.

"Once you have a good product," he said, "the key is marketing. Word of mouth is not enough by itself. A reputation has to be cultured the way Maytag did it. You have to send your beer to the right people, get the right personalities to write about it."

Reich is not concerned about the ethics of pasteurization as are some micro-brewers. He thinks the beer actually tastes a bit better when it is pasteurized because the sugars are very slightly cooked, giving the beer a somewhat mellower and richer flavor. He is disturbed that many people who don't balk at paying $3 a bottle demand that it be served at 33° F. "Those people don't care what it tastes like."

Reich expects to sell 4,000 barrels in 1983, 6,000 in 1984, and 8,000 in 1985. He also hopes someday to buy a building near his office and construct a 25,000–30,000-barrel brewery of his own. Reich's idea made great sense—commission an established brewery to make the beer to his specifications. If the beer didn't sell, the investors, including himself, had only lost a year's cash flow, not the much larger sum needed for a plant and equipment.

After my tour of Newman, Anchor, New Albion, and New Amsterdam I remained enthusiastic but was more respectful of the difficulties involved in being a small brewer. All four brewers loved good beer. All recognized the importance of marketing and the insatiable demands of small business. I admired all of them for different reasons: Maytag because his beer was the best; McAuliffe because he had built his brewery out of nothing but sweat and determination; Newman because he had so much faith in the English-style ales to which I was partial; and Reich because he was so pragmatic about marketing.

All four American brewers had nourished my fantasies. At the same time, they gave me a clearer understanding of some of the difficulties and challenges of brewing. I was ready for some serious study.

A Savage Commitment

For several months, I continued to dream of building my own brewery. The last brewery in Vermont, Petersen's in Burlington, had closed its taps in 1894. It was time for a successor. With Vermont's established reputation for good cheese and maple syrup, the state begged to have a small brewery offering real ale or real lager. Not only would the residents love the beer, but the fifty million people living within a day's drive would surely thirst for a Green Mountain brew. Once I had the tourists hooked, they would do my marketing for me, carrying the message and the demand home to Massachusetts, Connecticut, New York, and beyond.

Everyone with whom I spoke thought the idea was terrific, but talk was cheap and I knew I couldn't do this alone. I needed to find other people who were as serious as I was. Therefore, I invited a selection of friends over one evening to pursue the idea of building a small brewery. They were all people who liked my beer or who were home brewers themselves. They included a lawyer, an investment advisor, an engineering student, a contractor, a community organizer, Barton the hot tubs entrepreneur, and the former manager of a whey-processing plant who had become a food equipment broker.

For an hour the conversation ranged across possible names for a brewery, types of beers, location, cost, and customers. I glorified Anchor, New Albion, and Reich's rental-brewery scheme. I told them of the micro-segmentation in the market and the growth of imported beer sales and home brewing. The more home brew we drank, the better the idea seemed. But during a pause in the jollity, Jim Hinkel, the equipment broker, asked to speak. He said he had scribbled a few notes just before the meeting and wanted to share them.

"First, I think you need to define the reasons for the venture. Is this to be a hobby or a business? Will it stand alone or be part of something else, such as a pub or a restaurant?

"Second, you must lay out the financial factors in pro formas for at least three years. When do you expect a profit? How do you plan to raise the money? Have you talked to any banks?

"Third, there are marketing factors. Where will your beer fit into the present market? What share do you expect to get in Vermont, in New England, in three years, in six years? Who are your competitors, and what are their strengths? Are you challenging Budweiser, or Genesee, or Heineken? What is your sales plan? You need at least a three-year unit pricing forecast. What promotional programs do you have in mind?"

I gulped and looked around the room. The others were squirming, too, but Hinkel wasn't finished.

"Fourth, there are construction factors. What are the state and federal regulations on building a brewery? Have you looked at the taxes? A brewery is very capital intensive. What size will you build? Can you find the equipment off the shelf or must it be custom-made? What is your construction budget? Whatever you calculate here, you can count on doubling it.

"Fifth, what are your personnel requirements? How will they be trained and what will you pay them?"

Hinkel paused to catch his breath. "These are just a few notes. I haven't even touched on financing, distributors, suppliers, utilities, etcetera, etcetera."

The etceteras tolled like a clock on Death Row. The message was clear: he wasn't telling us to go back to the drawing board; in his opinion, we hadn't even entered the drafting room.

After I had recovered from Hinkel's cold shower of realism, I realized that I should probably not discuss a brewery over beer. It was also obvious that far more serious study was called for. I started plowing through some of the brewing industry textbooks. I inquired about brewing schools and found out which small breweries took on apprentices. I read trade journals. I talked to every micro-brewer I could find.

I tasted domestic and foreign beers with a more discriminating and critical palate. The quality was decidedly various. Some were good and some were worse than my own—sulphury, cidery, or stale. I also learned that of the first ten micro-breweries in the country, four had already shut down.

Saddest of all was the demise of New Albion. Jack McAuliffe was unable to get his production and consistency up to profit-making levels, and he couldn't raise the capital to expand. A couple of people in the industry said he was perhaps his own worst enemy because of his erratic quality and self-delivery. This was dismaying news, for I sensed that no one had worked harder than McAuliffe. For the home brewer dreaming of his own brewery, the closing of New Albion was like the death of a prophet. Making a profit at brewing was far more difficult than just making good beer.

There was another lesson here. In all the newspaper and magazine articles I had read about New Albion and the other micro-breweries, none had hinted at marketing, distribution, or consistency problems. Reporters were content to write glowing feature stories about brewers who time and again used almost identical words: "We're selling all we can make!" It was Jim Schleuter of the River City Brewing Co. in Sacramento, California, who finally broke that bubble. "When has any of us ever sold all we could make? You know we all lie." It seems that the reporters clouded their normal skepticism with the romance of beermaking and a tiny-is-beautiful philosophy. One brewer who had made the above claim to a reporter, admitted to me six months later that he'd been forced to throw out half a year's production because the batches were contaminated.

There were other failures.

Charles Coury of the Cartwright Brewing Co. in Portland, Oregon, believed that his seventeen years of producing wine would make brewing "as easy as falling off a log. I guess I was a little arrogant. The differences in degree were so great they became differences in kind, but I didn't recognize that for a long time.

"I wish we could have labeled the beer Brew Number 1, Number 2, etcetera, and then on the back of the label asked for comments. Everyone expected the first beer to be perfect. I would have been better served spending a year making home brew while I built up my cash flow. In retrospect, it takes quite a bit of wasted beer to break in the equipment and get the right taste." After a year and a half and $100,000, the Cartwright operation closed.

Fred Eckhardt, who acted as an informal advisor to Coury, commented, "The things he wanted to do, he didn't have the equipment for. The things he should have done, he didn't recognize the need for. So he went more than a year trying to solve technical problems and competing with people he shouldn't have been competing with. The people he should have been selling to want something different. They want a taste that says 'Love me or hate me.' He finally got around to changing the formula and it was pretty good. But by then it was too late."

My own best beer is a stout, black as obsidian, chewy as porridge, and bitter as Guinness. However, I know the audience for it is small and it would never attract many buyers. I rate Fritz Maytag's Anchor Steam Beer as the best in the country, but it took him years of careful, persistent, exhausting selling to convince people to buy it.

Still, hopes (or is it hops?) spring eternal. When the American Homebrewers Association expanded its annual convention to include micro-brewing, scores of people traveled to Boulder, Colorado, for lectures on malt and brewing traditions, equipping a brewery, mashing theory, and hops utilization. David Bruce flew in from London to talk about his brew pubs. Other speakers discussed styles of beer, packaging, the production of malt extract, and we all took a tour of the biggest mega-keggery in the world, the Coors plant in Golden.

At one session I asked how many people had come primarily for the micro-brewing information, and fully half the audience raised their hands. Some had visited Anchor, which at 25,000 barrels was no longer a micro-brewery, and other small operations. In experience and savvy, the group ranged across the spectrum from glassy-eyed hippies out of the mountains to a Virginia veterinarian who brewed so frequently that he had refrigerated an entire room for storage and was now trying to raise $200,000 for the giant step into commercial production. Between sessions, the talk was all of two-row versus six-row malt, how to find and convert dairy equipment cheaply, whether to make ales or lagers, and where to build.

At the end of the conference, when Fred Huber of the Huber Brew-

ing Co. (300,000 barrels) said he would do whatever he could to help any nascent micro-brewer, I thought the whole audience would bolt forward to take up his offer.

At the second conference a year later, the general level of sophistication and realism was noticeably higher.

In the following pages, I will set down the major constituents necessary to build a micro-brewery. These ideas are based upon conversations with a dozen brewers across the country.

First, the micro-brewer must realize that brewing involves all the agonies, long hours, constant decisions, and financial balancing acts of any small business. After the television cameras and the reporters have left, the bills must still be paid. "People get caught up in the romance of being a brewer," said Jim Schleuter of River City. "They forget that brewing is really just a business, and if you don't like business, or can't make it pay, you're sunk."

"We found that making the beer, despite its difficulties, was the easy part, maybe fifteen percent of the business," said one of the founders of the Boulder Brewing Co. in Colorado. "Forget the romance of experimenting with different kinds of hops and malts. You've got more important things to think about, like keeping the beer free of bacteria and then selling what you make."

The micro-brewer can easily fall into the trap where he believes that the beer will somehow sell itself. It's good for him to imagine himself making cardboard boxes or spark plugs or computer chips as an antidote to the romance of beer.

What to Brew

The question of what to brew is paradoxically complex.

Dozens of prospective micro-brewers have taken courses in fermentation science from Michael Lewis at the University of California at Davis. When he poses this question to them, most reply, "Oh, a beer like Beck's or Heineken." For Lewis, this is not nearly good enough. A brewer must believe that his is the best possible beer he can make, for that faith will be needed to elbow out the dozens of competing brands.

Should he make an ale, porter, stout, or lager? Most home brewers are drawn to the darker, heavier, English-style beers because they are so clearly different from the bland, clear, pale American lagers. Most micro-brewers have chosen ales, porters, and stouts because they are relatively easier and cheaper to make than lagers and because they can command the high import prices. American beer drinkers are inured to the taste of light, clear, cold lagers. Why should the micro-brewer try to compete with that style? What's more, ales mature faster, and at higher temperatures, thus obviating the need for more expensive refrigeration and aging equipment. Finally, the stronger taste of darker beers can cover more off-flavors than light lagers. With a light lager, there is no place to hide your mistakes.

Only one of the micro-brewers I visited made lager—the River City Brewing Co. Theirs is the superb River City Gold, which ranks just below Anchor Steam as my favorite American beer. Jim Schleuter has taken on the big American brewers at their own specialty and beat them hollow.

Will the beer be tank-conditioned or bottle-conditioned, filtered or not filtered, pasteurized or not? In the early years of the micro-brewery movement, most brewers (excluding Maytag) proclaimed the purity of their "living" beer and made a virtue of necessity by asserting that the yeast layer in the bottom of the bottle and the slight cloudiness of the brew were marks of distinction. There are limits to these claims. Sediment might impress some beer drinkers, especially home brewers, but most Americans drink with their eyes as well as their mouths. More importantly, as any serious all-grain home brewer knows, living beer is unstable and very susceptible to contamination. Pasteurization didn't become popular because of a desire to kill taste but to kill infection.

I'll wager that if you gave most micro-brewers the money to buy a filtering system or a pasteurizer, they would accept it. River City has used a filter from the first batch. It is nothing more than a converted swimming pool filter, but it works—both River City Gold and Dark are crystal-clear in the bottle.

Having formulated your special recipe, you must now decide how to serve it. There is a debate among micro-brewers over the relative merits of bottles or kegs. Home brewers who become micro-brewers are inclined to recall the tedium of cleaning and filling hundreds of bottles and prefer the simplicity of kegs. Bottles require a bottler and a labeler, both of which are expensive, hard to find, and harder to maintain. Packaging is another expense that most brewers don't count on. If the brewery is in a state with a deposit law, the cost of cleaning or buying new bottles could wipe out a small profit.

However, there are at least three problems involved with selling draft beer in kegs. Name recognition is harder to develop. Most bar customers simply ask for a "draft," not a specific brand. Then they drink the beer out of an anonymous glass. Draft drinkers tend to want a beer that is cheap, cold, and clear, and may not be willing to pay extra for a fuller taste. Second, it is more difficult to get a bartender to try a new keg than a new bottle. "Which of my three or four drafts am I supposed to pull out to install yours, Mr. Micro-Brewer?" The distributor of the displaced brand will not bow out gracefully. Every new account will be a struggle. Third, for every keg actually being tapped, the brewer needs six to eight more in the production cycle, for cleaning, filling, aging, and in transit.

William Newman built his brewery on the premise that Albany's high consumption of draft beer would sustain a kegs-only production. However, after one year in operation, he decided he needed the higher profit margin of bottles, and he offered 30 percent of his company's stock to raise $100,000 to underwrite a bottling line. He admitted he had learned a "hard lesson."

There are three perspectives from which to launch a micro-brewery.

The first is that of the home brewer who scales up his hobby to commercial proportions. He thinks incrementally of batches ten or a hundred times the size of his basement operation. Often he will do much of the construction and fabrication himself. New Albion, Boulder Brewing, and Thousand Oaks (Berkeley, California) belong to this class.

The second category includes brewers who may or may not have been home brewers, but who think of their operation as a scaled-down big brewery. This classification is as much an attitude as a matter of equipment. If they can find used commercial equipment, they buy it. These brewers are aware of the fragility of beer, and they understand why the big breweries go to such pains to maintain sanitary conditions. They waste no time or energy damning the major brewers. They have no illusion that their beer will displace Dos Equis or Kirin or Beck's.

Two members of this group are a hundred miles apart—River City in Sacramento and the Sierra Nevada Brewing Co. in Chico, California. Whereas Jim Schleuter of River City makes a fine hoppy lager, Paul Camusi and Ken Grossman produce bottle-conditioned pale ale, porter, and stout. The two breweries don't compete directly, but they both aim to be second only to Anchor. The two plants are very different in style and operation. Whereas Camusi and Grossman (both former home brewers) use stainless steel at every turn, Schleuter built most of River City himself out of what materials he could afford, which at first did not include stainless steel. He had never been a home brewer, but having worked for Schlitz, he knew the care the big brewers took over sanitation, and he kept his plant as clean as Camusi and Grossman's.

These brewers who scale-down possess another trait of the big brewers. They are ready to share information with other brewers. They are not secretive and they don't take pot-shots at their competition. "There are no secrets in brewing," said Schleuter, "only your mistakes."

A subspecies of the scaled-down breweries are those built from kits by brewery manufacturers such as Hansbrew, Ringwood, or Bruwell, a subsidiary of David Bruce's Firkin chain. These companies, either English or German, have built dozens of breweries in Europe and have packaged turnkey operations of all sizes.

Contract brewing is the third path to micro-brewing. It has been practiced for some time, both in respectable forms—purchase of excess capacity for special brews—and in the more notorious forms such as Billy (Carter) Beer or Nude Beer. Matthew Reich was the first of the micro-brewers to take this route. His contract with F. X. Matt to make five-hundred-barrel batches of New Amsterdam to his specifications was "the smartest thing I ever did. You absolutely must figure out how to sell your beer first and create that market. You can always hire a brewmaster to make it for you and, if you're lucky, find a brewery to produce it. But if you can't convince people to buy the beer, there's no point in making it."

Using another brewer's excess capacity and generosity, however, works only until the host brewer asks himself why he should be making a super-premium beer that sells so well for someone else. That's the special nightmare of a brewer like Reich, which is why he continues to look for money and a location in Manhattan.

The micro-brewer who is not a former home brewer has one great advantage as he begins. He may lack an initial understanding of the technique of brewing, but he will also be far less romantic or ego-involved with the beer itself. He will not automatically equate initial effort with final goodness. Home brewers who turn commercial are often mesmerized by equipment or taste and don't realize how much time and money they must spend to sell it. One micro-brewer told me in a fit of self-delusion, "Why should we advertise our beer? People ought to pay for the privilege of selling it." Such warm self-esteem will never offset the chilly indifference of the marketplace.

Where to Learn Brewing

Micro-brewers have taken several paths to brewing competence. Some, like McAuliffe at New Albion, taught themselves through books and experience. Others, like Reich and Maytag, took brewing courses. Jim Schleuter of River City spent two years working for Schlitz, and William Newman served an apprenticeship at the Ringwood Brewery. Other Americans have worked at Paine & Co. in Britain. Formal courses in brewing are offered at the U.S. Academy of Brewing in Stamford, Connecticut, the Center for Brewing Studies in Boston, and the Siebel Institute in Chicago. A few universities, notably the University of California at Davis, give courses and grant degrees in Fermentation Science.

Even before he opened his brewery, Newman was besieged by people who dreamt of doing the same. Both to structure those "consultations" and earn some extra money, he began to offer two-day courses in brewing. For $300, his students spend the first day brewing a batch and the second listening to Newman "de-romanticizing the brewery business." Newman said that no one else was offering this kind of exposure to reality. Several people told him that by paying the $300 they had saved themselves $300,000 for the real thing.

Skills

At its simplest, Jack McAuliffe said, brewing means turning water into money. However, there's more to it than that. The brewer depends on hard, practical science and technology to turn out the same good beer week in and week out. Unless he is wealthy enough to pay someone else to run the brewery, he must have or learn a range of crafts. The brewer who starts from scratch must be a cross-breed of pack rat, junk dealer, shade-tree mechanic, and surgeon, who slavers over food equipment magazines the way others read *Playboy*. At the same time, he needs what Paul Camusi calls "that indefinable feel for brewing." Some people are born cooks while others, no matter how many cooking courses they take, have tin tongues.

When asked what kinds of skills the prospective brewer needs, Jim Schleuter said, "Electrical work (three-phase wiring), plumbing, welding, tile work, carpentry, refrigeration, mechanical ability, and all-purpose cussing. Those mechanical skills must be in the blood. By the time you're an adult, you don't have time to learn all these things." Schleuter and his wife, Chris, started River City with $40,000 in savings. He knew enough about metal and hydraulics to design and subcontract work he couldn't do himself. For $5,000 he bought a dilapidated bottler and rebuilt it into a $30,000 asset.

The small brewer must know pumps, piping, flow rates, and be able to size and repair equipment. Sierra Nevada and River City both have complete machine shops on the premises where the brewers fabricate much of their own equipment. The brewer must know the difference between cold zone and hot zone equipment and understand that sanitation must be fanatically maintained in the former.

Costs

How much will the brewery cost? That depends of course upon how large it is, how much beer you expect to sell, how many other businesses you own, how big a salary you want, and a host of other factors. After three years in operation—and an investment of $150,000—the two owners of Sierra Nevada broke even and were paying themselves salaries of $175 per seventy-hour week. In 1981, Schleuter said, "With first-rate skills, a good bottle-conditioned brewery using alternative technology might cost $100,000, but you'd really have to hit the scrap heaps to do it." By 1983 his bottom estimate was $250,000, still assuming that the brewer did a lot of his own work.

Some prospective brewers think that with the closing of over seven hundred American breweries in the last thirty years, used equipment at 10 cents on the dollar ought to litter the landscape. Perhaps this was true twenty-five years ago, but today most defunct breweries have been bought and brokered and are pumping beer for Brazilians, Nigerians, and other Third World imbibers.

Newman and Reich both raised an initial $250,000, but spent it in dramatically different ways. Newman channeled his money into a building and brewing equipment, while Reich put every extra penny over the cost of his contract with F. X. Matt into marketing. In England, Tom Litt built his hundred-gallon brewery for $10,000, but it was only one part of his three-legged income. Fritz Maytag said the industry average capital cost per barrel installed capacity was between $100 and $200 and for a micro-brewery it would be closer to the higher figure.

From my discussions with these brewers, I think $250,000 is a rock-bottom figure for anyone who wants to build a free-standing brewery that will provide a living wage. Stuart Harris, the former small-breweries editor at *Zymurgy*, believes even this is too low. Certainly, the cost of real estate, local health requirements, etc., will also affect the total.

Finally, the brewer should remember the prediction of Jim Hinkel: whatever he calculates as cost will eventually double.

George Peppard in Easthampton, Massachusetts, gathered the following figures for a projected 4,000–12,000-barrel brewery in 1982.

START-UP COSTS

Equipment	$175,000
Leasehold improvement	15,000
Installation	50,000
License & permits	7,000
Deposit/utilities	1,000

START-UP COSTS

Deposit/phone	$ 260
Deposit/rent	1,600
Operating Capital	50,140
TOTAL	$300,000

Equipment costs broke down as follows:

Malt-handling	$ 5,000
Spent grains	2,000
Mash/lauter tun	7,000
Hot water tanks	4,000
Brew kettle	25,000
Fermenters (4)	20,000
Storage tanks (2)	8,000
Wort cooler	8,000
Beer hose	3,500
Filter unit	10,000
Boiler unit	10,000
Refrigerator unit	7,500
Beer barrels (1,000)	40,000
Barrel washer	5,000
One-arm racker	5,000
Lab & cleaning equipment	15,000
TOTAL	$175,000

The brewery should be big enough to make all the beer you expect to sell. Ross Heuer, the former editor of *Brewers Digest*, contends that a micro-brewer needs to sell 10,000 barrels annually to be comfortably self-sufficient as well as a force in the market. Lending weight to his judgment, in 1983, both Sierra Nevada and River City acquired the equipment to reach that capacity. As Schleuter remarked, "At ten thousand barrels I will no longer be a micro-brewery and I can send the hopefuls to these other tiny operations." Paul Camusi told a *Wall*

Street Journal reporter, "At our current level of two thousand barrels, we're so small it's ridiculous."

Marketing

After spending several years designing a formula, raising the money, finding a location, scrounging for equipment, and living on macaroni and cheese, the new brewer might be forgiven for believing that the beer will be an instant success without advertising. Just a few newspaper articles, a television spot, and presto! the newest kid on the block whips everyone else. But the real street corners of the market are far less hospitable or forgiving.

Too many of the early micro-brewers either didn't allocate money for marketing or expected the beer to create its own demand. The brewer must meet the customer more than halfway. He must find the right niche in the market, price the beer intelligently, and create an image before the sale. As has been said for all sorts of products besides beer, the real competition is anything chosen in preference to your own.

"There's a big market based on snobbishness out there," observed Michael Lewis. "These beers represent the same image as BMW cars, alligator shirts, and Perrier. It's not a fickle market so long as people think they get their money's worth. The alligator shirt happens to be an extraordinarily hard-wearing shirt. People are not fools. If they pay a buck a bottle for Boulder Beer and it's very good, they'll say, 'I know something. I'm getting a real gourmet kick for my money.' If the beer is less than good, then they'll drink something else. That's something a lot of the hopeful brewers don't understand. They think they need only to make something better than Budweiser."

If hopeful micro-brewers want further confirmation of the need for sophisticated marketing, they should listen to Robert Pohl, executive vice-president of the "small" million-barrel Hudepohl Brewing Company in Cincinnati. "We are not in business to sell beer; we're in business to sell image. If you are selling [just] 'beer,' you're in serious trouble." The cost advantage on producing ordinary beer today is overwhelmingly with the giant brewers and even operations of Hudepohl's size cannot compete. "The long-term salvation of the small brewer is to produce a high-quality beer for sale at a high price." This is exactly what the Huber Brewing Company did with its Augsburger brand. In eight years, its proportion of Huber sales rose from less than 5 percent to over 30 percent. The only major caveat Pohl offered was that if the brewery already has a weak image and tries to leap into the premium or superpremium market, the customers will simply laugh.

Distribution

Once the beer is bottled or kegged and sitting on the loading dock, how will you get it to the retailer? After the repeal of Prohibition and the end of the tied-house system in the United States, there developed the so-called three-tiered system of brewer-distributor-retailer. As breweries have become fewer and bigger, they have sought to reduce the number of distributors they deal with. The smaller regional breweries have had a harder time finding distributors and competing with the huge contracts of the national brands. The plight of the micro-brewer is even graver. In the first place, he must convince the distributor that the product is worth his while. Distributorships are not philanthropic institutions and they are not cheap. For their cut, some take as much as the brewer keeps. Also, as Fred Huber observed, "The micro-brewer has to find a distributor with imagination and those are few and far between."

Some micro-brewers have signed up with distributors of imported beers, others with distributors of wines. Still others, like McAuliffe and Newman, have opted for self-distribution. Maytag agrees that self-distribution makes sense where the brewer himself may initially call upon accounts and develop good rapport and name-recognition. But once those are well established and the beer moves into more distant markets, he needs to sign up a distributor.

Regulations

Beer is a regulated drug. Like it or not, when you make and distribute beer, federal, state, and local officials have a special interest in you. If you don't like regulations and rules, you probably shouldn't be brewing beer.

As far as I can tell, the federal Bureau of Alcohol, Tobacco, and

Firearms is interested primarily in your criminal record—if you are a convicted felon, you may not brew—and your willingness to pay the $7 per barrel in federal tax. Other than that, they seem to be quite cooperative.

Every state has its own alcohol regulatory agency. The microbrewer must also please the state in other matters such as health codes, manufacturers' fees, etc. Local jurisdictions usually control such factors as zoning and building permits.

Jim Schleuter made up a list of the permits and licenses he needed before opening in California:

County and/or City Requirements

1. Name permit and publication (also known as "dba")
2. Environmental impact report
3. Approval of neighboring owners within 500 feet of each corner of the brewery
4. Approval of landlord/owner if brewery is not owned by principals
5. County Board of Supervisors' approval
6. Building inspection
7. Health inspection

State Requirements

1. Alcohol beverage manufacturer's license
2. Label approval
3. State Board of Equalization for seller's bond and beer excise tax permit

Federal Requirements

1. Bureau of Alcohol, Tobacco, and Firearms
   a. Brewer's bond of $1,000
   b. Tax rates
   c. Operational reports
   d. Occupational stamp
2. Employer's ID number from the IRS

Where to Build

Where the brewery is housed is not nearly as important as how. Both River City and Sierra Nevada are located in nondescript, standard metal-frame buildings on the outskirts of Sacramento and Chico, California, respectively. Yet for all micro-brewers, brick holds a powerful attraction, especially if they want to use the structure to help promote the romance of tradition. Brick conjures up images of the sprawling Victorian factories where stout men in moustaches, derbies, and suspenders made real beer.

At least this was my dream as I drove around Burlington and adjoining Winooski looking at possible sites. Both cities were in the middle of an economic renaissance, and developers were rapidly buying up abandoned fabric mills for conversion to apartments and shops. Good places to put a brewery, I thought.

However, the most picturesque location for a brewery was eight miles south of Burlington at Shelburne Farms, a one-thousand-acre remnant of a four-thousand-acre Victorian estate on Lake Champlain. Three magnificent buildings remain on the grounds—a house and two European-style barns. One of them, The Farm Barn, is a massive, five-story structure with cupolas, copper roof, and brooding, dark brown shingles. A perfect place for a brewery. The estate is now controlled by Shelburne Farms Resources, Inc., a nonprofit corporation which experiments with different farming ventures such as a dairy, bakery, and cheese factory. They also have several fields planted to barley. Perhaps they could raise hops as well? Then we would have a totally self-sufficient industry and a great marketing ploy.

I went to the manager and laid out my half-serious proposal. He gave me a curious look and said, "This is the second time in six months I've been approached with that idea." The other proposal came from two Germans—a brewmaster and a financier—and an American investor who wanted to spend over $1 million at Shelburne Farms. They intended to buy a used German brewery and bring it to Shelburne. They planned to grow some of their own hops and malt on the farm and produce up to 50,000 barrels per year, about twice the amount of Maytag's 1982 production. In three years, they predicted, their beer would capture 10 percent of the Vermont market. (At that time, Molson held 4.5 percent after ten years of hard selling.) Furthermore, they hoped to employ twenty to twenty-five people.

Their arrival on the scene was a shock. Great minds may think alike, but I had not considered such a large and expensive operation. If these fellows were serious, this was hardball, not slow-pitch softball. Thus, I received my second involuntary cold shower. Obviously, the state was not big enough for two micro-breweries.

More importantly, I had to ask myself one more time: Did I really want to build a big factory like this, or did I simply want to watch people order my beer, smack their lips, and put their money down on the table with an appreciative "That's real beer"? Did I have the technical and managerial skills to oversee construction, let alone the brewing? Did I have the marketing flair, money, and moxie to sell my beer when all about me were doubting its value?

In the end, I realized I had no more business in commercial brewing than I had in professional bagpiping or full-time beekeeping or running marathons every couple of weeks. I didn't think I could raise the $500,000 for a real try at success. I knew I didn't possess the mechanical ability to run pumps and bottling lines. Finally, I was not conscientious enough to maintain the operating-room cleanliness needed to make uncontaminated beer month after month.

The words of Michael Lewis came back to me: "The ones who make it in this business will be extreme characters. The work is extraordinarily hard, and those who don't give a hundred percent won't get to first base. You can't plan to work sixty hours a week and take Sunday off. This is a seven-day job if you build from scratch. (If you have so much money that a brewery would be built as a tax loss, it's a different story.) To be successful, the micro-brewer must have a savage commitment to every aspect of brewing and selling. What's more, it really helps if that person has already run a business, both for the experience and for the ability to borrow against that other business.

"For every hundred people who think about building a brewery, ten will try it and only one will succeed."

And Fritz Maytag warned, "To be a brewer, you must have nightmares regularly. You've got to think about the problems all the time."

Still, the vision of a brewery would not go away. My mind turned to Britain's fifty-odd brew pubs. I thought also of how Tom Litt had made a success of his Lilliputian brewhouse. The profit from his hundred gallons a week was a solid third of his income, and the brewing took only one-seventh of his waking hours. What's more, he did it with extracts, something any home brewer could relate to. No distributors, no marketing, no table tents or T-shirts. No worry about bottles or distribution. This seemed like a good compromise.

In this dream I was not alone. Steve Morris, my co-conspirator in the state home brew championships had similar fantasies. He hoped to convince members of the Cram Hill Brewers to build a club brewery, which would provide beer for its members and sell the surplus. That idea only lasted a few months—until they realized that too many brewers would surely spoil the beer. I knew that Bill Owens had already raised almost $70,000 for a brew pub in Livermore, California. The Vermont Liquor Control Board told us it was possible we could sell the beer at the brewery for on-premise consumption. This would be, in effect, a brew pub.

A brew pub was also attractive because it would give daily access to the customers. No need for elaborate market research. Just ask your friends what they would like to buy.

Brew pubs are a favorite idea of Tom Burns, a former brewmaster at Boulder Brewing Co. "A lawyer by chance, a brewer by choice," Burns thinks that brew pubs, assuming they are legal, might have a brighter future than micro-breweries. In 1982, at least a half dozen states permitted multiple licensing so that a manufacturer could also sell on premise.

With a brew pub, the owner would not risk his entire shirt just selling beer. Construction costs might range from $40,000 to $70,000, not five to ten times that as for a free-standing brewery. On the other hand, operating a brew pub puts you in the restaurant business as well as the brewing industry. A brewery in a brew pub may be only one of three legs on the financial stool, but together those legs must be strong and balanced and someone has to worry about all three.

Burns pointed to the California statute covering brew pubs as simple and easily adaptable to other states. According to the California Business and Professions Code, Sec. 23357: "Licensed beer manufacturers may also sell beer to any person holding a license authorizing the sale of beer and may sell beer to consumers for consumption on the manufacturer's premises owned by the manufacturer which are contiguous to the licensed premises and which are operated by and for the manufacturer."

Once again, between the simplicity of this language and the passing of similar legislation in other states lies a long struggle of education and lobbying. There are no automatic allies in this battle—not the distributors, not the bar owners, probably not the restaurateurs or the average beer drinker. Lobbying for more drinking outlets in times of rising concern about alcoholism will not be easy.

In the meantime, the Shelburne Farms brewery was still-born. A falling-out between the partners sent the brewmaster back to Germany. Three months later, when I heard of another brewery proposed for a town on the Vermont-Quebec border, I was unmoved. The truth had sunk in—my most compelling motivation for owning a brewery was to have immediate, face-to-face public recognition and gratitude for my beer. Now that my beer had improved so much, I received these blessings for my home brew. To turn that exchange into money would cheapen it and be *very* expensive for me. Even a brew pub was more work than I wanted.

Far better, I concluded, to stick to home brew.

Home to Home Brew

The decision not to build a brewery simplified my life and allowed me to again take uncomplicated pleasure in the hobby of home brewing. The hobby had became part of my annual routine. Like a farmer adjusting to the seasons, I brew a ten-gallon batch every five or six weeks, except during the hot months of July and August. I consume these batches at the rate of one or two bottles an evening, and hold the remainder as presents and for guests.

Building a brewery was the logical extension of home brewing only in fantasy, not in fact. When I realized all that was required to become a commercial brewer, I was reminded of a passage from Harold Blaisdell's book, *The Philosophical Fisherman*, in which he describes a pastime with all the fun squeezed out of it:

> A man can become so caught up in fishing that it actually becomes a grim business, and when this happens, it is time to slow the tempo and take a breather. It is time . . . to shift his attention from the fish and focus it upon himself. If a fellow can do this, if he can sit quietly for a day and do nothing more pretentious than keep half an eye on a bobber or the tip of his rod, he will see many things that he has been missing. . . . If he obtains the proper state of objectivity, he will see in himself all the ludicrous qualities which make him the human being he is.

I didn't need to apologize for my efforts. I have come a long way in ten years of brewing. That none of my bottles explode is only the most superficial accomplishment. That the beer no longer tastes cidery is only slightly more positive. My beer is now well balanced, full bodied, and fresh. Even the imports taste dull in comparison to my better brews. I have four or five standard recipes down pat, and I experiment with the rest. I make a full range of beers, from the delicate, flaxen-hued pilsners through the ales to the robust, carbon-black stouts. I have a beer for every mood and every occasion: hearty, warm stouts to accompany shepherd's pie in winter; light lagers served cold for the end of a summer day's run. Today, the only outside beers I drink are my friends' home brews, beer I've never tasted before, any micro-brewery product, Guinness, Pilsner Urquell, and Anchor Steam.

Are my beers better than Bud or Heineken or Beck's? I certainly think so. Yet that question, which once seemed so vital, has faded into insignificance because once I decided not to venture into commercial brewing, I found my antipathy toward the big brewers weakening. My short intellectual fling at commercial brewing gave me deep respect for the technical abilities of the big brewers. They are very good at producing a pale, clear, balanced beer. They can make any beer they want, which is something that cannot yet be said for most micro-brewers. They choose to make a beer aimed at the most common denominator because it is simply more profitable to make a product that both truck drivers and debutantes will enjoy. That's fine. If that's what people want to drink and brewers want to make, why should I worry? Big Brewer does not bar the path to good home brew. So what if Miller is owned by a tobacco company? Why should it bother me that Budweiser uses a lot of rice and tastes thin?

Home brewing is very much like cooking in its practice and its rewards. The ambitious cook is driven by a mixture of discipline, freedom, and pride; the same is true of the serious brewer. He uses other people's recipes as training ropes before cutting free to find his own path. Like good cooks, most home brewers, even those making a "house" brand, are never quite satisfied with their product.

After pleasing yourself, the joy of home brewing comes from pleasing others. That satisfaction takes several forms. One friend, an extremely accomplished physician, cellist, and painter, never liked beer—until I brought some of my lager to a dinner party she gave. She tried it and now says my beer is the only kind she will drink.

A different judge was friend and brewing mentor Hal Boutelier. He has brewed for fifteen years, painstakingly teaching himself through scores of one- and two-gallon batches. He's filled a dozen notebooks with recipes and continually experiments with different equipment. He now makes the best pale ales and lagers in Vermont. One day I took a bottle of my best lager to test his reaction and steeled myself for indifference—or worse, rejection. When he said he could detect no off-flavors, and pronounced the beer "quite respectable," I was overjoyed.

Most home brewers love to convert an ordinary beer drinker into a brewer. Peter Bergh already had a taste for imported beer when I began sharing my beer with him in payment for some of his spring water. As the months passed, he took a greater liking to my brews (and even said so) until he joined the brew club, bought the equipment, and made his first batch. With clean equipment, supervision, and a little beginner's luck, he produced a good extract ale the first time around. From the moment he opened the first bottle of that first batch, he was hooked. In the next month he brewed four more batches, and he seemed to call every other day for advice and reassurance.

Much of the credit for the improvement in my beer, I confess, must go to the overall improvement in home brewing materials and techniques. When I started brewing, Prohibition-era methods were the rule. A few lucky brewers had access to English malts and hops. For the rest of us, Blue Ribbon malt, cane sugar, and baker's yeast were choices akin to Henry Ford's color options for the Model T: "Any one you want so long as it's black." English malt companies and other suppliers have moved aggressively into the American trade with dependable products. As demand grew, wholesalers also found supplies of domestic hops, although only one or two American companies have tried competing with the English maltsters.

Given this increased demand and supplies, there is much loose talk among home brew retailers about the coming "explosive growth" in home brewing, as one of them put it. They and other enthusiasts point to the dramatic increase in retail supply stores, since the legalization of home brew in 1979. They think specialty beers and home brewing will gain the following of the small winery and homemade wine business of the last ten to fifteen years. *Zymurgy*'s Charlie Papazian estimates there are between 300,000 and 500,000 people who brew with some regularity. No one really knows because there are no statistics.

I am skeptical of so much optimism. There are so many other enticements for people's time, from windsurfing to rock climbing to Chinese cooking. Another reason I don't think home brewing will explode is that home brewers work best alone. It is not a hobby you share with your friends except at club meetings or when you give beer away. In that sense it is very much like beekeeping. Home brewing is a good complement to other hobbies such as running, tennis, or cooking.

If a huge increase in the number of home brewers does occur, it will be caused either by a dramatic improvement in the quality of the brewing kits and a spectacularly adroit marketing campaign, or a skyrocketing in commercial beer prices. Economy now motivates only a small minority of American home brewers, and these tend to be Prohibition-style brewers. After all, a six-pack of inexpensive beer can cost less than six cans of cola. This was not true twenty years ago.

Home brewing will continue to attract the same kind of people who belong to our club—individuals with the taste and funds for imported beers, but the curiosity, pride, and adventuresomeness to make their own Beck's or John Courage. Any home brewer now has the means to match almost any brand of commercial beer provided he counts his emotional involvement. Home brewers drink first for taste, second to slake a thirst, and last to get a buzz.

All home brewers are missionaries, and as one I hope that all serious beer drinkers will try to brew their own at least once. Realistically I know this will never happen. Many of those hundreds of thousands of people who buy home brewing kits may not even use them more than once. The poor quality of many kits is partly to blame for this. Retailers or manufacturers, hoping to lure first-time brewers often assemble equipment and materials based solely on cost. They load up on the dextrose and aged hops which tend to produce cidery, unpalatable beer. I'd like to see kits that would introduce customers to an all-malt brew. They'd cost more but give more satisfaction.

Home brewing also does not occur in a vacuum. Its future depends upon the future demand for specialty and imported beers and the micro-brewery industry. Import sales will continue to grow, but not at the pace of the last ten years. American brewers are responding with their own "super-premiums" and pouring money into promotion.

As for the micro-breweries, it seems unlikely that they will multiply as quickly as wineries have in the past two decades. Beer, unlike wine, is process-oriented rather than ingredients-oriented. That is, the technological and capital requirements of brewing are substantially greater than for winemaking. Beer is more fragile and needs more careful handling. No one talks about "operating-room cleanliness" in a winery. (On the other hand, vineyards require land and a certain kind of climate.) Many people run vineyards and wineries as part-time jobs because much of the work is seasonal. This would be impossible in a full-scale brewery. I would hope that in another ten years there will be ten to fifteen solidly grounded micro-breweries in this country with another three or four score struggling imitators.

Home brewers will probably be some of the most appreciative customers for micro-brewery products, but they are too few to spell the difference between red and black ink. One micro-brewer said he appreciated home brewers' support, then added, "But I sure wouldn't stay open a week if I had to rely primarily on what they buy."

The four-thousand-member American Home Brewers Association has launched a Campaign for Better Beer modeled on the British Campaign for Real Ale. *Zymurgy* defines one goal as "education and care taken by the brewmaster and the brewery management, by the home brewer, the grower and supplier of ingredients, distributor and the beer drinker who can distinguish if beer has been cared for."

Lacking in this country, however, is an outraged sense of loss and a wide understanding of what is being lost through consolidation, that is, traditional, cask-conditioned ale. In the United States, "real lager" disappeared long before Prohibition, and most of the remaining small breweries have chased after Millerweiser's dominating bland style. This makes it almost impossible for great numbers of beer drinkers to formulate a rescue plan. Far better, I think, for serious beer drinkers to lobby (in the broadest sense) for the maximum varieties of beer, be they imports, home brew or the micro-brewery brews.

In this book I have celebrated home brewing. Its practitioners belong to a ten-thousand-year-old tradition that includes Sumerian peasants, German braumeisters, English brewsters, and George Washington. Beer was once one of the world's great folk beverages. Only during the last few decades has it become the indistinct, bland, highly carbonated drink most people buy as an afterthought in a bar or the grocery store. Through their diligent and creative labors, modern home brewers can help to restore beer to its proper place as a great food and art form.

Making your own beer is full of paradoxes. To "have a beer" is synonymous with relaxation, yet brewing is a matter of hard work and concentration. Beer is the surpassing drink of companionship and conviviality, yet it is best made in solitude. You brew to suit your own taste, yet your greatest satisfaction comes in sharing it with others. The more you make, the more you savor each sip and swallow. The corollary to this last observation is that when you make your own beer, you probably drink less than you would otherwise.

Beer still suffers from its association as Archie Bunker's champagne. Similarly, mental hangovers from Prohibition-style home brew to this day deter many beer drinkers from trying to brew their own. That is a great pity. Modern home brew is as different from its Prohibition-era ancestor as Beefeaters is from bathtub gin. Moreover, the average home brewer has an immense variety of beers he can make. Just as there is a wine for every mood and occasion, so there is a beer. Shouldn't that beer be the tastiest, most delicious, most lovingly crafted beer around—*your* home brew?

Cheers!

Appendix 1: Recipes

Grand Rapids Lager

4 lbs. light dried malt extract
2 lbs. dextrose
5 gals. water
1½ oz. Hallertau hops pellets, of
    which ¼ oz. is for aroma

2 packets bottom-fermenting
    yeast
1 cup dextrose (priming)

Bring 1 gal. water to boil. Turn off heat. Add malt and 2 cups dextrose. Stir well.

Bring back to boil for 20 minutes, then add 1¼ oz. hops. Boil another 40 minutes. After about 20 minutes, take 1 cup liquid and force-cool to 75° F. Add 2 packets yeast to make starter.

About 5–10 minutes before end of boil add last ¼ oz. hops for aroma. Turn off heat. Let stand for 10 minutes.

Fill primary with 2–3 gals. cold water. Add wort and rest of yeast. Add water at temperature to give final temperature of 60°–65° F. Take a hydrometer reading if you're curious. It should be 46–48. (This recipe calls for a primary and secondary fermenter, but you may also use the blow-by system. See Chapter 7.) Cover the primary with lid. After 2 days, or when the foam peaks, carefully skim off the scummy crown with a sterilized spatula or spoon.

When gravity has fallen to about 1020 (about 5 or 6 days) transfer to sterilized secondary fermenter. Attach fermentation lock, and cover with dark plastic. When bubbles come less frequently than one per 90 seconds, siphon beer to clean carboy or primary , add 1 cup dextrose dissolved in boiled water, and bottle. Beer may be drunk in 3 weeks, better after 2 months.

Original gravity: 1044–1047; final gravity: 1010–1014

One other thing Nichols taught me was how to pour beer properly. Yeast sediment is a fact of life for home brew. It is good for you, being laced with B-vitamins, but it will cloud the beer if the bottle is shaken. Therefore, if you want to drink clear beer, you must pour it carefully, all at one time. To leave the sediment in the bottle, incline the (uncapped) bottle so that the beer flows into a tilted glass. Stop when the yeast sediment just begins to move toward the spout.

If you don't care about clarity, and want a bigger dose of B-vitamins, just pour the entire contents, sediment and all.

Sap Beer

4 lbs. dried malt extract,
    light or dark
1 qt. maple syrup
5 gals. water
2 oz. Hallertau pellets, of which
    ½ oz. is for aroma

1 tsp. Irish Moss
2 packets bottom- or top-
    fermenting yeast

Follow directions for Grand Rapids Lager, except that Irish Moss should be added 30 minutes before the end of the boil.

The great difference in this beer is its taste. If you have ever boiled your own maple syrup and burned some of it in the pan, this beer will remind you of that smoky flavor.

This is a variation on a colonial recipe that used maple sap as the basic ingredient for beer. It is not cheap—a quart of syrup can cost $6 to $9, but it's so tasty.

Home Brewing
Is a Metaphor for Life Ale
(Amber Ale)

Any combination of 6–7 lbs. malt extract, liquid or powdered (e.g., a can of light syrup and 3 lbs. dark dried malt

1 lb. crystal malt

2 tsps. gypsum

1 tsp. noniodized salt

1½–2 oz. Northern Brewer or Bullion hops pellets for bittering

½ oz. Hallertau or Cascade pellets for aroma

5 gals. water

2 packets top-fermenting yeast

1 cup dextrose

Boil 1–1½ gals. water. Add gypsum and salt, then turn off heat. Add malts. Boil 20 minutes, and then add half the bittering hops.

Withdraw 1 cup wort. Force-cool to 75° F., and add 2 packets yeast to make yeast starter. Cover.

Boil 20 minutes, add rest of bittering hops, and boil 20 minutes more. Turn off heat. Add aromatic hops, and let stand 10 minutes.

Put 2–3 gals. cold water in clean carboy. Add yeast starter. Add gallon of cold water to wort to bring temperature below 150° F. Siphon wort into carboy for total of 4–4¼ gals. This will reduce the amount of liquid blown out the tube. Attach blow-by and follow directions for other beers.

I do not take a hydrometer reading with this concentrated brew.

When the foam has stopped moving along tube (about 2–3 days), pull off tube, add water to make 5 gals., attach a fermentation lock, and let the brew ferment flat.

Bottle with 1 cup of dextrose or dried malt extract dissolved in hot water as priming sugar. Age 3–5 weeks.

Final gravity: 1014–1016

Boneshaker Stout

6 lbs. dried malt extract, dark
5 gals. water
½ lb. black patent malt
1 lb. flaked barley
1 lb. crystal malt
2 oz. Bullion hops pellets for
    bittering
½ oz. Cluster or Cascade hops,
    fresh loose if possible, for
    aroma

1 tsp. noniodized salt
1 tsp. Irish Moss
2 packets Edme ale yeast or
    other top-fermenting yeast
1 cup dextrose or dried malt
    extract for priming

Bring 1½ gals. water to boil. Turn off heat, and add salt and malts. Bring back to boil for 20 minutes, then add 1 oz. Bullion. Boil another 20 minutes, and add 1 oz. Bullion and 1 tsp. Irish Moss.

Withdraw 1 cup wort, force-cool to 75° F., add yeast, and cover. Boil another 20 minutes, then turn off heat. Add aromatic hops, stir, and let stand for 15 minutes.

Put 2–3 gals. cold water in carboy, and add yeast starter.

Strain wort into another vessel, using 1–2 qts. hot water to sparge flaked barley, which will be thick. Siphon wort into carboy, giving good rousing.

Follow directions for Metaphor Ale.

Take hydrometer reading, which should be about 1050. Attach blow-by. Allow to ferment until flat—about 2 weeks at 60° F. Transfer to clean vessel, add priming sugar, and bottle.

I've drunk this in 10 days, but it's better to practice deferred gratification and wait 3–4 weeks.

Ma Vlast Lager
(5-Gallon Mashed)

9–11 lbs. pale malt grain
8½ gals. water
½ lb. crystal malt, cracked
3 tsps. gypsum
2 oz. Saaz or Hallertau pellets for bittering
½ oz. Saaz or Hallertau pellets for aroma

1 tsp. Irish Moss
2 packets bottom-fermenting yeast (I prefer Vierka)
Gelatin (optional)
1 tsp. ascorbic acid at bottling time (optional)
¾ cup dextrose for priming

Add ground grain and 3 tsps. gypsum to 10 qts. water at 126° F. Hold between 118°–125° F. for 45 minutes. Raise temperature to 155° over the next 20 minutes.

Meanwhile, heat 6 gals. water to 170° F. for sparging. Hold for 25–30 minutes, or until iodine test shows starch is converted. Raise temperature to 168°. Hold for 5 minutes.

Transfer grains to mash bucket, and sparge to recover total of 6 gals.*

Boil wort 25 minutes. Add 1 oz. bittering hops, and boil another 25 minutes. Withdraw 1 cup to make yeast starter. Add Irish Moss and remaining 1 oz. bittering hops, then boil another 25 minutes. Turn off heat. Add aromatic hops, and let stand for 20 minutes. You should have boiled off almost 1 gal. in steam.

Strain wort into a separate vessel, stir, and let stand 5 minutes. Force-cool this wort to 75° F., either with wort chiller or by standing it in a tub of cold water. Siphon into carboy, adding yeast starter half-way through.

Take hydrometer reading. Original gravity: 1045–1050; final gravity; 1010–1015.

Follow blow-by and bottling instructions as for other beers.

---

*You may want to take a hydrometer reading at the end of the sparging when you have collected 6 gals. If your reading is less than 1030, you can still add 1–2 lbs. dried malt extract to make up for either bad malt or an incomplete sparge. A little white lie is better than a thin beer.

The Gang's All Here Ale
(10-Gallon Batch, Half Mashed)

9–11 lbs. pale malt grain
10 gals. water
3 lbs. dried malt extract, light
3 lbs. dried malt extract, dark
1 lb. crystal malt
2 tsps. Irish Moss
4 packets top-fermenting yeast
4 tsps. gypsum

Gelatin (optional)
4 oz. Cascade or Fuggle pellets
   for bittering
1 oz. Cascade or Fuggle pellets
   for aroma
2 packets gelatin
1½ cups dextrose or dried malt
   extract for priming

This recipe combines mashing and extracts. The first task is to mash and sparge the grain.

Mash the grain in 2½–3 gals. water at 125° F. Hold temperature between 118°–125° for 45 minutes. Raise temperature to 155° over the next 30 minutes, stirring all the while. Hold temperature at 153°–155° for another 45 minutes: this is the starch rest. Perform iodine test. If test is positive, raise temperature to 168° to kill enzymes.

During the starch rest, heat another 6 gals. sparging water to 170°. Sparge with whatever method you prefer to collect 6 gals. wort. Bring this 6 gals. sparged liquor to a boil. Turn off heat while adding dried malt extracts. Boil for 20 minutes, and then add 2 oz. bittering hops. Boil another 20 minutes, add rest of bittering hops, and boil 20 minutes more. Add Irish Moss, and boil 15 minutes. Turn off heat. Add aromatic hops, stir, and let stand for 30 minutes. You may want to strain this wort into another vessel.

During second half of boil, withdraw 2 cups of wort, force-cool it to 75°, and add 4 packets yeast. Cover.

You need 2 carboys for the next step. Pour 2 gals. cold water into each. Then, after cooling the wort through the wort chiller, add an equal amount to each carboy. Also divide yeast starter in half and add to each carboy partway through.

Original gravity: 1040–1044.
Final gravity: 1012–1015.
Proceed as for other recipes.

Appendix 2: Glossary

Adjuncts. Unmalted cereal grains (often in American commercial beer) added to barley to produce more, and usually cheaper, sugars. Common adjuncts are rice, corn, and wheat. For the home brewer, dextrose, or corn sugar, is the most common adjunct.

Aging. Or maturation, during which time the yeast drops out of the beer and the flavor changes to make beer smooth and mellow.

Alcohol. In beer is ethyl alcohol (C_2H_5OH), the preservative and intoxicating component in fermented beverages. Roughly half of the product of fermentation.

Ale. A beer brewed with top-fermenting yeast at warmer temperatures (60°–70° F.) Usually, but not always, a faster maturing beer.

Ascorbic acid. Good for colds, good as anti-oxidant in beer. Added just before bottling.

Black patent. Barley malt that has been kilned at 450° F. to produce a rich, roasted flavor. Generally used in stouts.

Body. A term to describe the fullness of beers, how they feel and taste.

Bottom-fermenting. Describes the type of yeast for making lagers which require colder fermenting temperatures and a slower process.

Brewing. The marriage of malt, hops, and water, through mashing and boiling.

Carbon dioxide. The gas given off during fermentation, roughly equal in weight to the alcohol produced at the same time.

Carboy. Large narrow-necked glass vessel, used as both primary and secondary fermenter.

Chlorine detergent. Powerful sterilant for all bottles and equipment. However, it can kill yeast, so containers and equipment must be well drip-dried or rinsed after using it.

Crystal or caramel malt. Malted barley which has been wetted while sugars are still in the grain, then dried at 250° F. to give a golden color and nutlike flavor to the beer. Used frequently in darker ales.

Diastase. The name for the combination of alpha and beta amylase enzymes that are released from the malt during mashing and that act to convert malt starches to malt sugars, dextrins, and maltose.

Fermentation. The process wherein yeast converts grain sugars into roughly equal parts of carbon dioxide and alcohol.

Fermentation lock. Also known as an air lock or bubbler; water-filled plastic stopper that during fermentation permits carbon dioxide to escape while excluding air (and thus contamination).

Finings. Substances, like gelatin or sturgeon bladder, used to clarify beer during secondary fermentation.

Flocculation. Coalescence and settling of the yeast cells during fermentation and aging, part of the process of clearing the beer.

Gypsum. Calcium sulphate, a salt used to harden water for making pale beers, especially pale ales.

Hops. For brewing purposes, the flowers of the hops plant, *Humulus lupulus*, which provide both bitterness and aroma to the beer. Since the essential oils, which provide the aroma, are lost in boiling, the practice is to add a portion of "aromatic" hops late in the boil or during fermentation, a process known as "dry hopping."

Hops pellets. Hops flowers that have been pulverized and compressed into pellet-form for convenience and preservation.

Hydrometer. A glass tube with lead or mercury ballast for measuring the specific gravity or density of a liquid compared to pure water. Pure water at 15° C. (59° F.) by definition has a gravity of 1.000. The hydrometer helps the brewer keep track of the progress of fermentation.

Irish Moss. A small amount of this refined seaweed added to the last part of the boil aids in assuring a clear beer.

Kraeusen (pronounced kroy-sen). The first foaming head of beer during fermentation. Also refers to the process of adding some fresh green beer to older aging beer to carbonate the latter naturally.

Lager. Beer fermented at colder temperatures for longer periods of time with a bottom-fermenting yeast. The predominate beer style throughout the world. From the German word *lagern,* "to store."

Light. May refer to body or color of beer. In the United States "light" is now synonymous with low-calorie beers such as Miller Lite.

Malting. The controlled germination of grain by careful steeping and drying to ready malt starches for conversion to sugars.

Mashing. The controlled steeping or soaking of malted barley to release enzymes which convert malt starches to fermentable and nonfermentable sugars.

Nonfermentables. The portion of the malt sugars that will not ferment and therefore add sweetness and body to the beer.

Original gravity. The original specific gravity of beer before fermentation begins. *See* Hydrometer.

pH. Measure of acidity or alkalinity of beer. Acidity increases (pH decreases) from mashing to boiling to fermentation and aging.

Pitching. Adding yeast to cooled wort to begin fermentation.

Porter. A dark, heavy, sweet ale, originally called "entire" because it was drawn from three different gravity taps. A favorite of the porters in London in the early eighteenth century, hence the name.

Potential alcohol. An estimate of the final alcohol content of the brew, based upon the measured sugar content at the beginning of fermentation. In all-malt beers, potential never becomes actual, because of the nonfermentable sugars in solution.

Priming. Adding a small amount of sugar to beer just before bottling to reactivate the yeast and thus carbonate the beverage.

Reinheitsgebot. The most important law relating to beer ever passed. The "Purity Law" of Germany, from 1516, decreeing that beer shall consist only of malt, hops, and water (the yeast was assumed).

Sparge. To wash out all soluble products from the mash prior to boiling.

Starter. A strongly fermenting yeast culture that gives a running start to the fermentation of a larger volume of bitter wort.

Steam beer. America's only original beer. Brewed first in ice-less California, steam beer is a lager fermented at ale temperatures. Called "steam" beer because of the lively head caused by kraeusening.

Stout. Dark, robust, full-bodied ale, the most famous exemplar being Guinness.

Top-fermenting. Describes the type of yeast used for ales and stouts, that is, one which works at warmer temperatures and faster speed.

Water treatment. The addition of certain salts, such as gypsum, to harden water for brewing.

Wort (pronounced wert). The liquid solution of malt sugars which forms the basis of beer. Sweet wort precedes the boil and lacks hops; bitter wort includes the hops.

Yeast. The *sine qua non* of beer; the microorganisms that give us bread, wine, and especially beer. In beer, they consume malt sugars and convert them to roughly equal portions of carbon dioxide and ethyl alcohol.

Yeast nutrients. Recommended in recipes where less than half of the sugar comes from malt. Unnecessary with higher proportions of malt because nutrients inhere in malt.

Appendix 3:
Brews and Breweries

My Favorite American Beers

1. Anchor Steam
2. Sierra Nevada Pale Ale
3. Huber's Augsburger

4. G. Heileman's Special Export
5. Catamount Amber
6. Red Hook Ale

Selected Micro-breweries and Brewpubs in the United States

Sierra Nevada Brewing Co.
   Chico, CA
Buffalo Bill's Brewery
   Hayward, CA
Mendocino Brewing Co.
   Hopland, CA
Marin Brewing Co.
   Larkspur, CA

San Francisco Brewing Co.
   San Francisco, CA
Boulder Brewing Co.
   Boulder, CO
Old Colorado Brewing Co.
   Ft. Collins, CO
New Haven Brewing Co.
   New Haven, CT

Tap and Growler
  Chicago, IL
D.L. Geary Brewing Co.
  Portland, ME
Wild Goose Brewery
  Cambridge, MD
Commonwealth Brewing Co.
  Boston, MA
Boston Beer Co.
  Jamaica Plain, MA
Santa Fe Brewing Co.
  Galisteo, NM
Manhattan Brewing Co.
  New York, NY
Columbus Brewing Co.
  Columbus, OH
McMenamin's
  Beaverton, OR
Hood River Brewing Co.
  Hood River, OR

Bridgeport Brewing Co.
  Portland, OR
Portland Brewing Co.
  Portland, OR
Philadelphia Brewing Co.
  Philadelphia, PA
The Vermont Pub and Brewery
  Burlington, VT
Catamount Brewing Co.
  White River Junction, VT
Virginia Brewing Co.
  Virginia Beach, VA
Hales Ales Ltd.
  Colville, WA
Redhook Ale Brewery
  Seattle, WA
Capital Brewery
  Middleton, WI

Bibliography

Books and Periodicals

Abel, Bob, *The Book of Beer* (Chicago, Illinois: Henry Regnery, 1976).

American Homebrewers Association, *Microbrewers Resources Directory* (A.H.A., Box 287, Boulder, CO 80306).

Baron, Stanley W., *Brewed in America* (Boston, Massachusetts: Little, Brown, 1962). Reprinted 1972 by Arno Press.

Berry, C. J. J., *Home Brewed Beers and Stouts* (Andover, England: Amateur Winemaker Publications Ltd, 1963).

Bravery, H. E., *Home Brewing Without Failures* (New York: Arc Books, 1966).

Brewers Digest, 4049 W. Peterson Ave., Chicago, IL 60646.

Briggs, Hough, Stevens, & Young, *Malting and Brewing Science*, 2nd ed. 2 vols. (London, England: Chapman & Hall, 1981).

Brown, Sanborn C., *Wines and Beers of Old New England* (Hanover, New Hampshire: University Press of New England, 1978).

Burch, Byron, *Quality Brewing* (El Cerrito, California: Joby Books, 441 Lexington Street, CA 94530, 1977).

Coe, Lee, *The Beginner's Home Brew Book* (Portland, Oregon: S.B. Taylor & Assoc., 1972).

Dunn, Michael, *The Penguin Guide to Real Draft Beer* (Middlesex, England: Penguin, 1979).

Eckhardt, Fred, *A Treatise on Lager Beers* (Portland, Oregon: Hobby Winemaker, 2758 N.E. Broadway, OR 97232, 1979).

Foster, Terrence, *Dr. Foster's Book of Beer* (London, England: A & C Black Publishers Ltd, 1979).

Hardman, Michael, and Theo Bergstrom, *Beer Naturally* (London, England: Bergstrom & Boyle Books Ltd, 1976).

Hooker, Richard J., *A History of Food and Drink in America* (Indianapolis, Indiana: Bobbs-Merrill, 1981).

Jackson, Michael, *The World Guide to Beer*, (New York: Ballantine, 1978).

Johns, Bud, *The Ombibulous Mr. Mencken* (San Francisco, California: Synergistic Press, 1968).

Kramer, Samuel, *The Sumerians* (Chicago, Illinois: University of Chicago Press, 1963).

Lender, Mark E., and James Kirby Martin *Drinking in America: A History* (New York: Free Press, 1982).

Line, Dave, *The Big Book of Brewing*, (Andover, England: Amateur Winemaker Publications Ltd, 1979).

Lundy, Desmond, *A Standard Handbook for the Production of Handmade Beers* (Victoria, British Columbia: Fermenthaus, P.O. Box 4220, V8X 3X8, 1979).

Master Brewers Association of the Americas, *The Practical Brewer* (Madison, Wisconsin: Impressions, 1977).

Miller, David, *Home Brewing for Americans* (Andover, England: Amateur Winemaker Publications Ltd, 1981).

Morison, S. E., *Harvard College in the Seventeenth Century* (Cambridge, Massachusetts: Harvard University Press, 1936).

Morris, Stephen, *The Great Beer Trek* (Brattleboro, Vermont: Stephen Greene Press, 1984).

Orton, Vrest, *The Homemade Beer Book* (Rutland, Vermont: Charles Tuttle, 1973).

Orwell, George, "Hop-Picking" in *An Age Like This*, volume 1 of *The Collected Essays, Journalism and Letters of George Orwell*, ed. Sonia Orwell and Ian Angus (New York: Harcourt, Brace & World, 1968).

Papazian, Charlie, *The New Joy of Brewing* (Boulder, Colorado: Log Boom Brewing, 1979).

Shales, Ken, *Brewing Better Beers* (Andover, England: Amateur Winemaker Publications Ltd, 1967).

What's Brewing. Monthly newspaper of Campaign for Real Ale; membership in CAMRA for £5 includes a year's subscription (CAMRA Ltd, 34 Alma Road, St. Albans, Herts AL1 3BW, England).

Zymurgy, Box 287, Boulder, CO 80306.

Articles

Davidson, Harold O., "The Bell Doesn't Toll for All Small Brewers," *Beverage World,* March 1981, pp. 29–33.

Eckhardt, Fred, "Talk to Your Beer," Amateur Brewer Bulletin No. 9, January 1983.

Eckhardt, Fred, "Hops," Amateur Brewer Bulletin No. 4, Fall 1977.

Hartman, Louis F., and A. L. Oppenheim, "On Beer and Brewing Techniques in Ancient Mesopotamia," Supplement to the *Journal of the American Oriental Society,* Number 10 (Baltimore: The American Oriental Society, 1950).

Pohl, Robert, "Can the Small Brewer Compete?" in *Brewers Digest,* January 1983, pp. 16–18.

Petri, Bill, "Malting your own Barley," *Zymurgy,* Special Issue 1981, p. 14.

Index

ABOUT THE AUTHOR

William Mares is the author of *The Marine Machine* (1971) and co-author of *Passing Brave* (1973), *Working Together* (1983) and *Real Vermonters Don't Milk Goats* (1984). A graduate of Harvard College and the Fletcher School of Law, he is a freelance writer who has contributed to *The Christian Science Monitor, The Economist,* and *The Chicago Sun-Times,* among other publications. A member of the Vermont state legislature, Mares has been a home brewer for the past fifteen years.

A NOTE ON THE TYPE

The text of this book was filmset in Aster, a type face designed by Francesco Simoncini (born 1912 in Bologna, Italy) for Ludwig and Mayer, the German type foundry. Starting out with the basic old-face letter forms that can be traced back to Francesco Griffo in 1495, Simoncini emphasized the diagonal stress by the simple device of extending diagonals to the full height of the letter forms and squaring off. By modifying the weights of the individual letters to combat this stress, he has produced a type of rare balance and vigor. Introduced in 1958, Aster has steadily grown in popularity.

Composed by Waldman Graphics, Inc.
Pennsauken, New Jersey.
Printed and bound by The Haddon Craftsmen,
Scranton, Pennsylvania.

Typography and binding design by Virginia Tan.